BIRDS & FLOWERS

Coloring Book for Adults

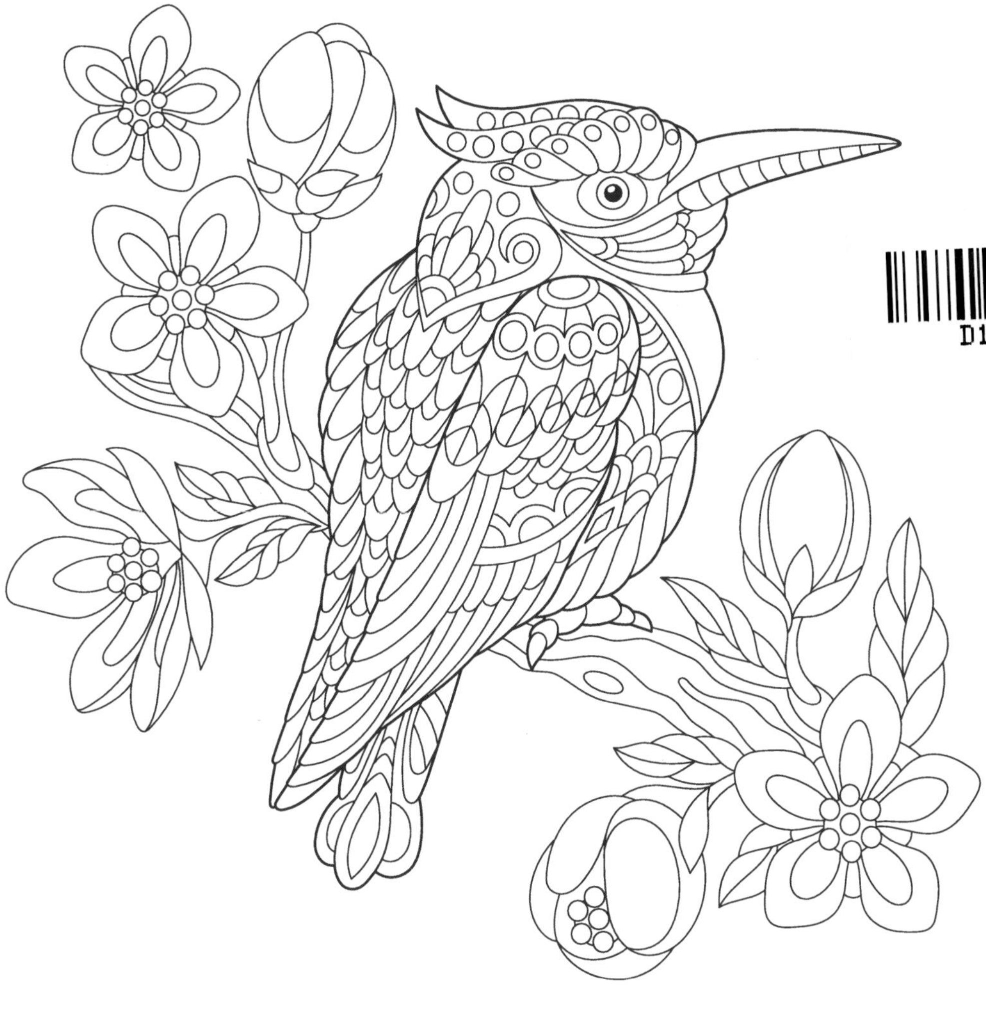

This Book Belongs to

Birds & Flowers Coloring Book for Adults

ISBN: 9798594007772

Printed in the USA

Color Test

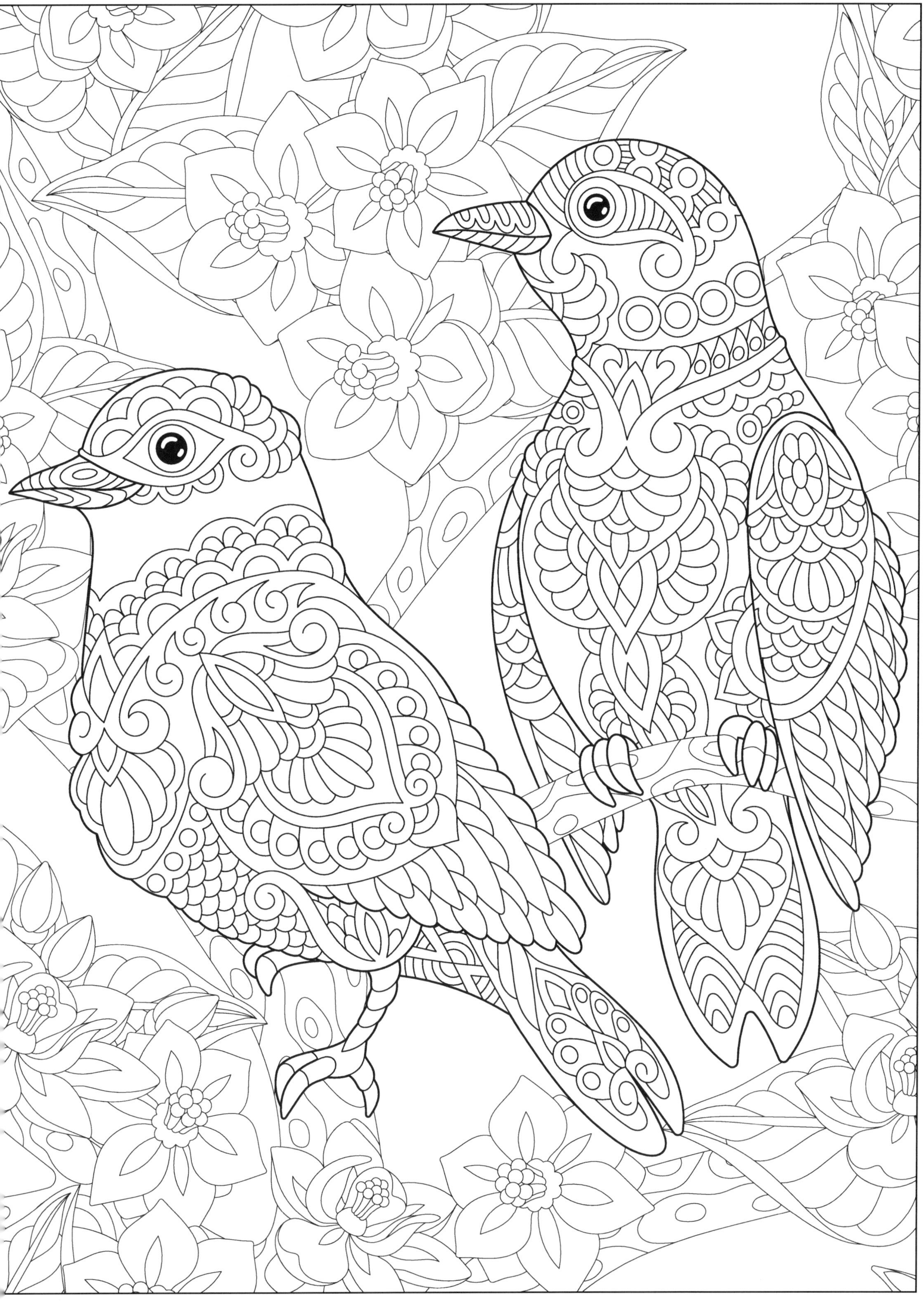

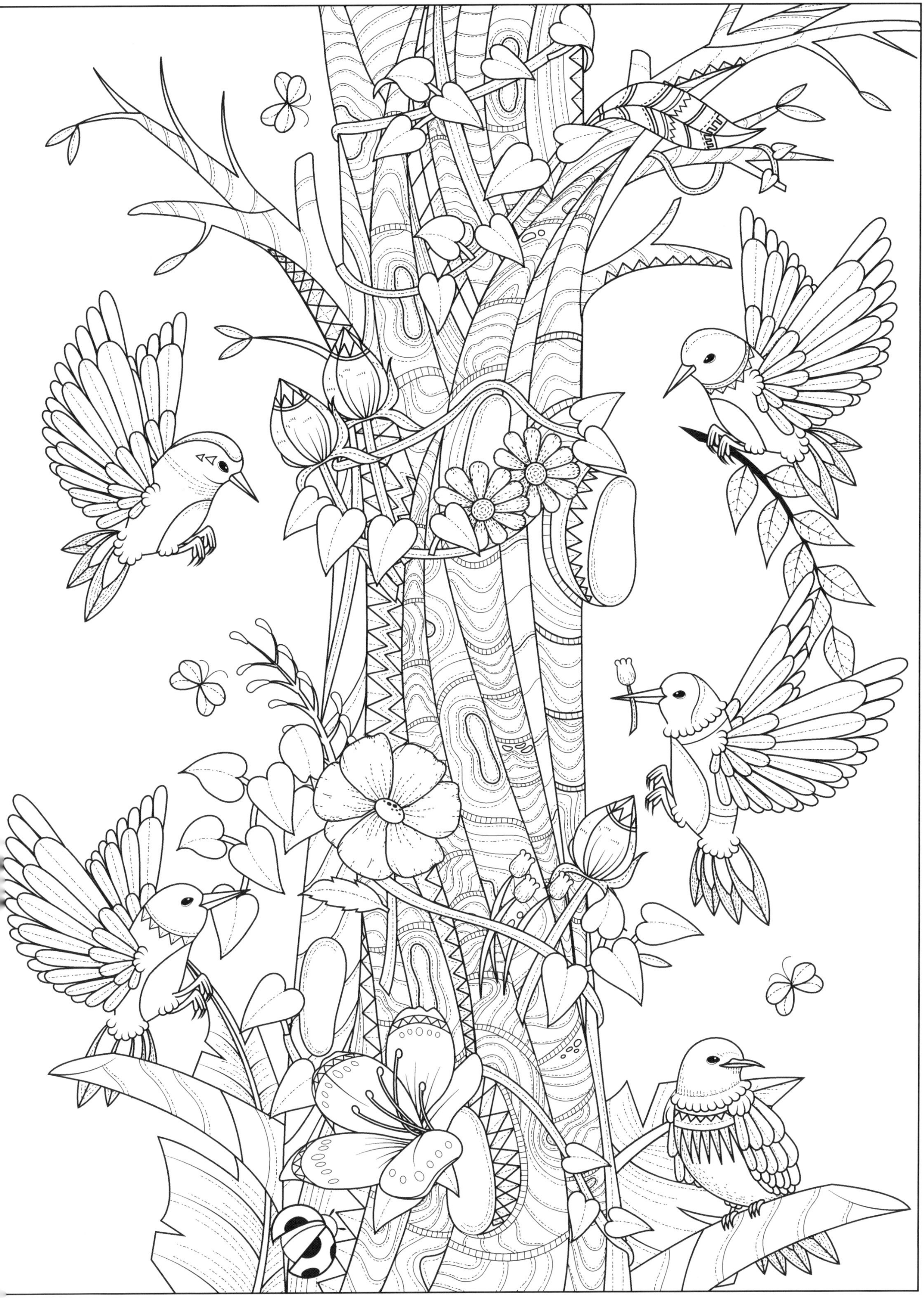

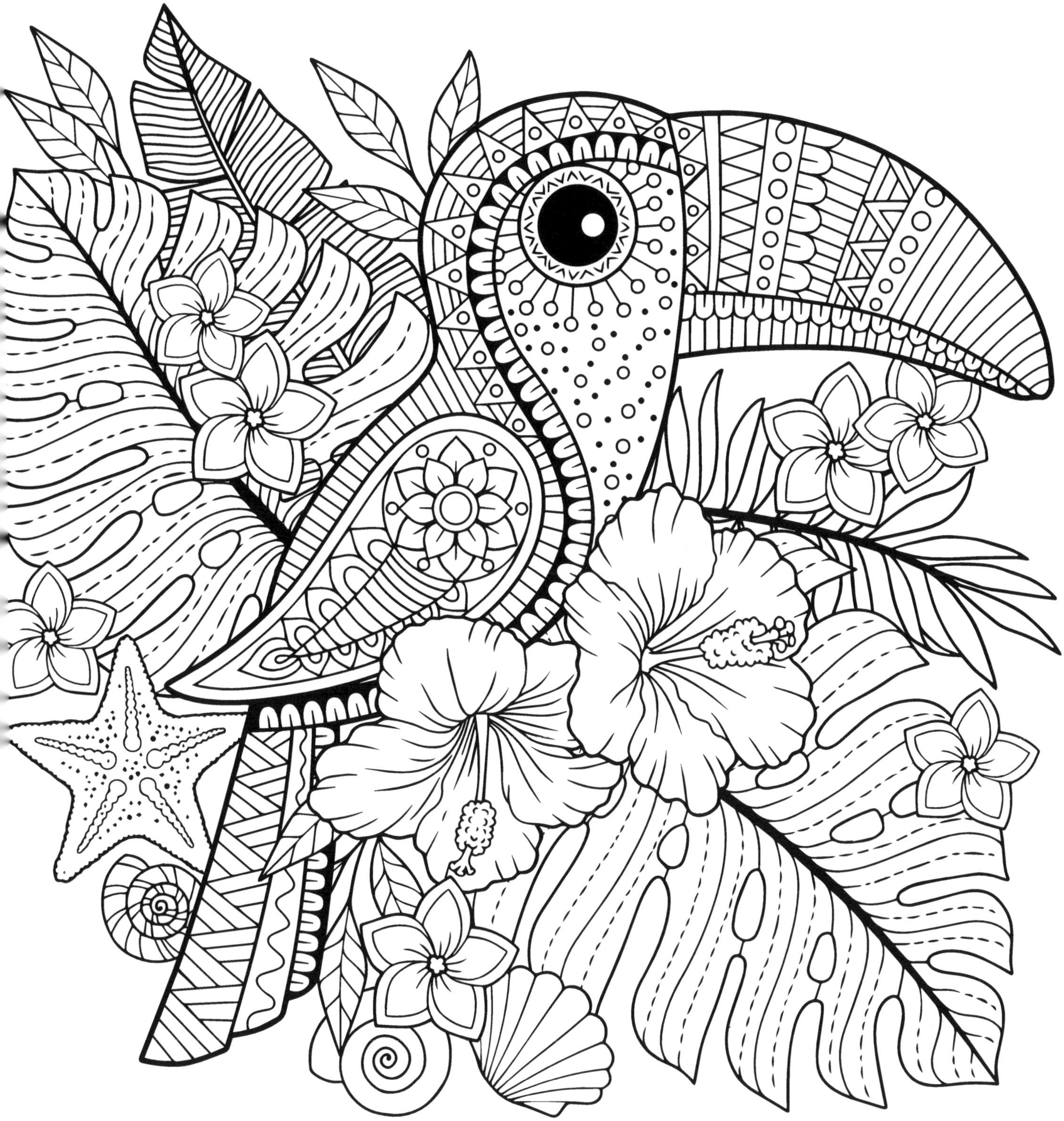

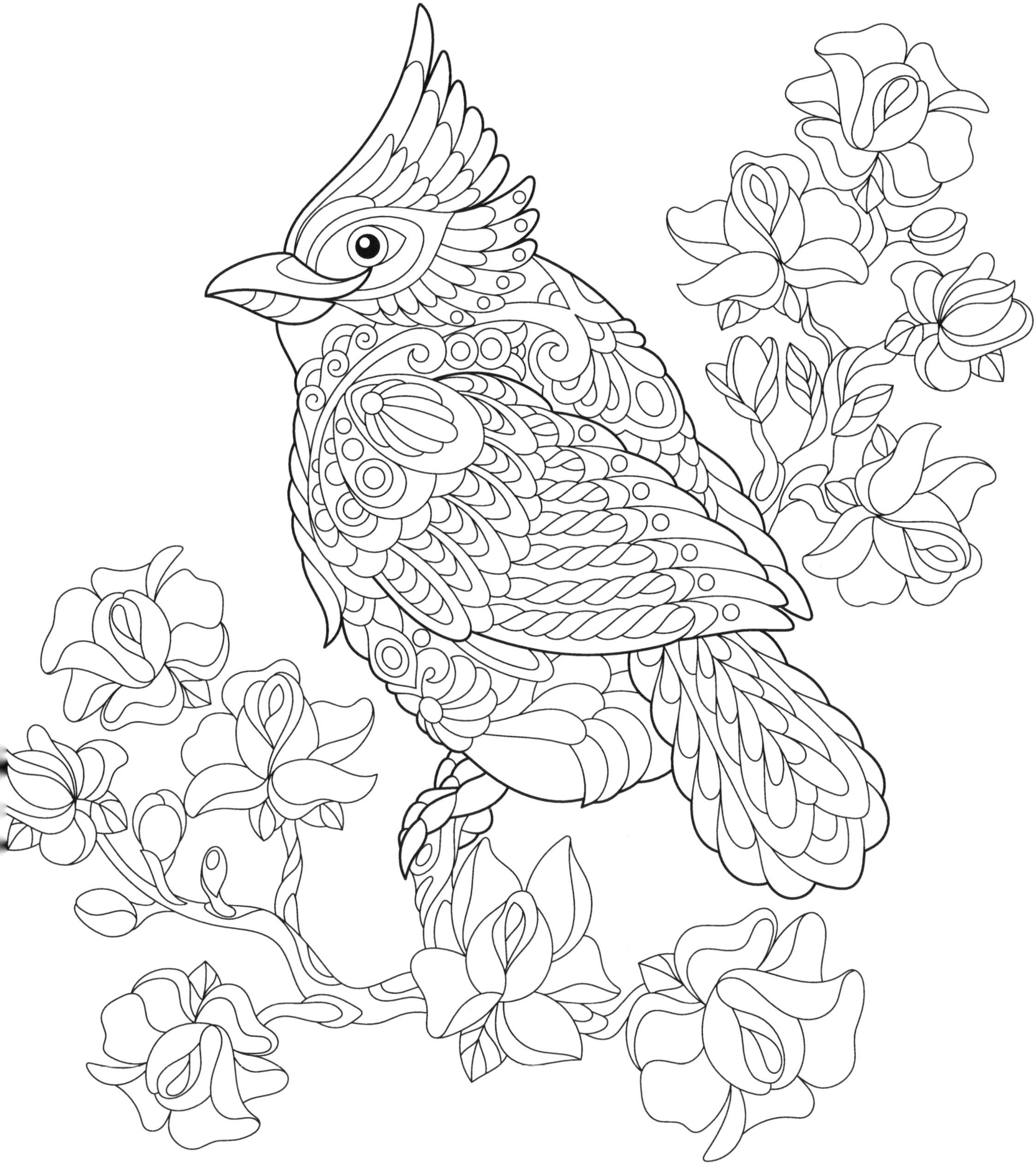

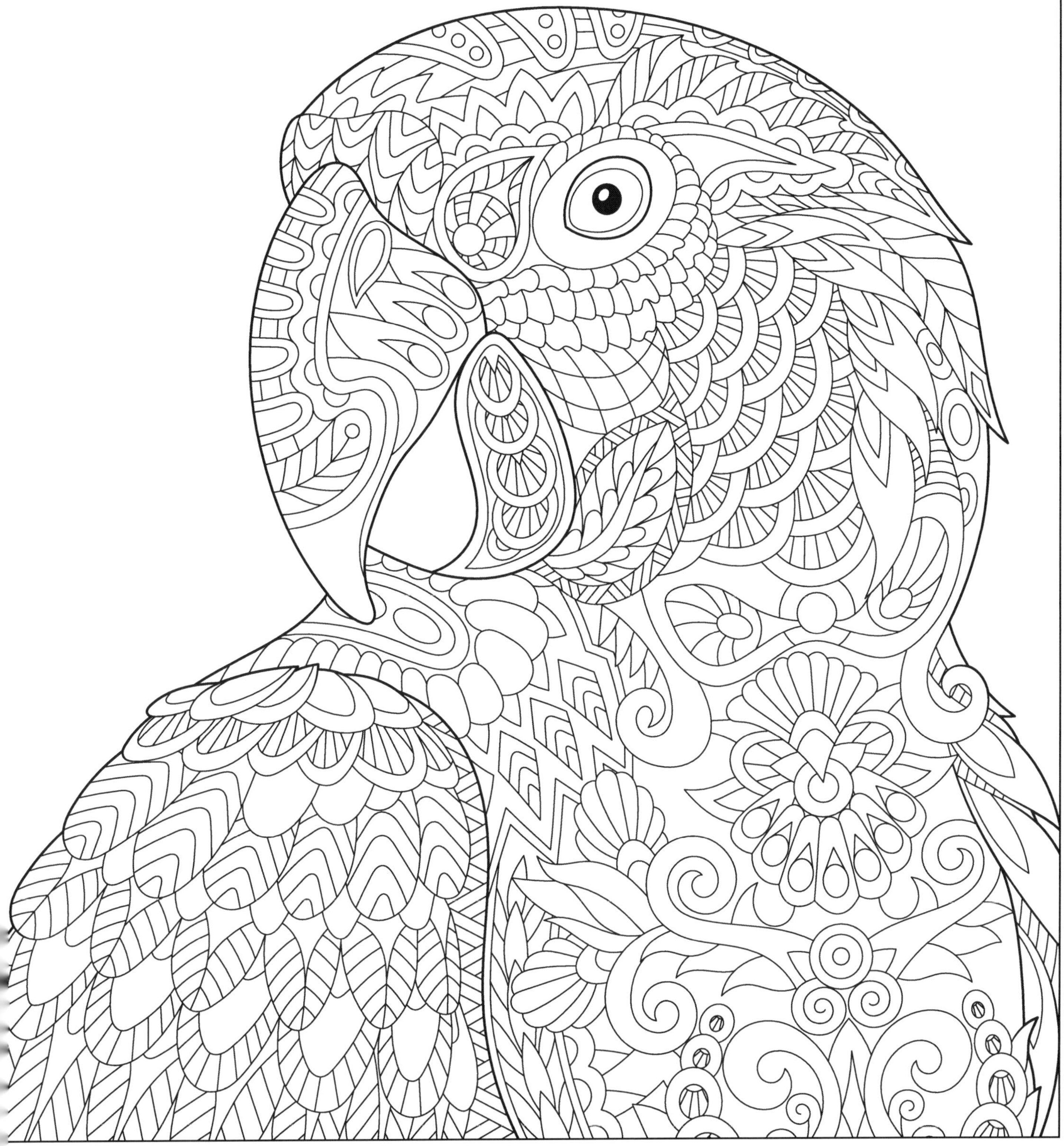

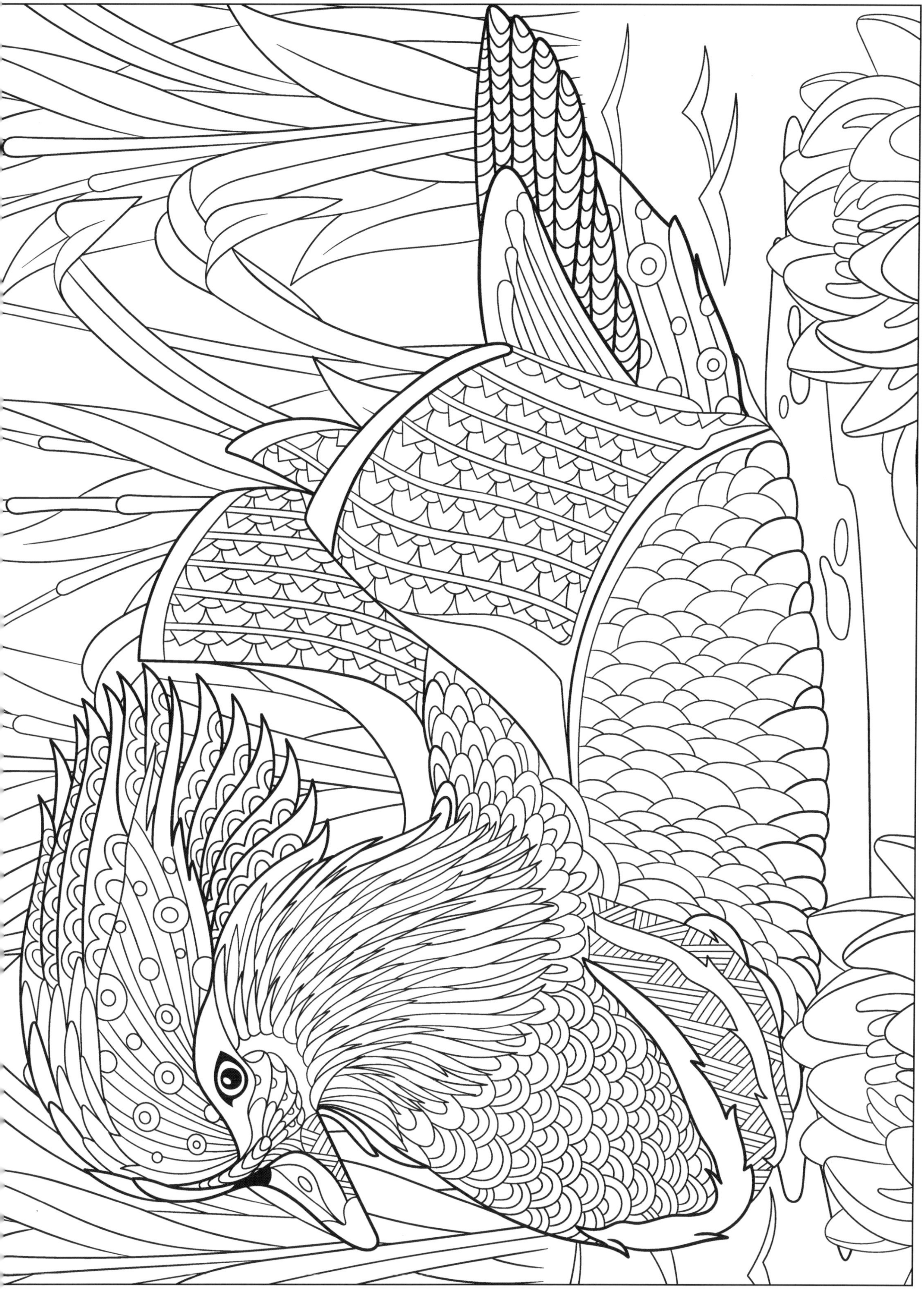

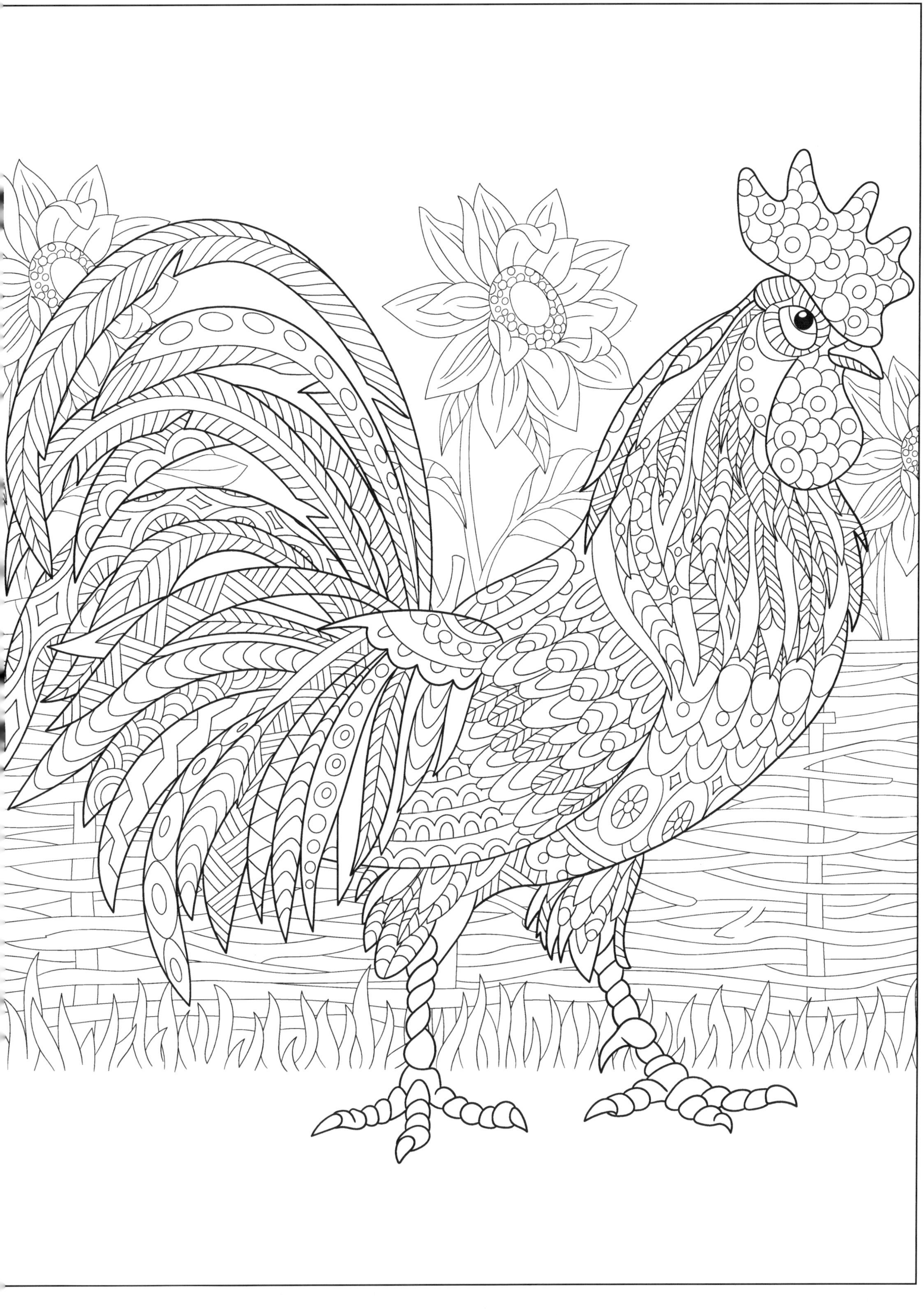

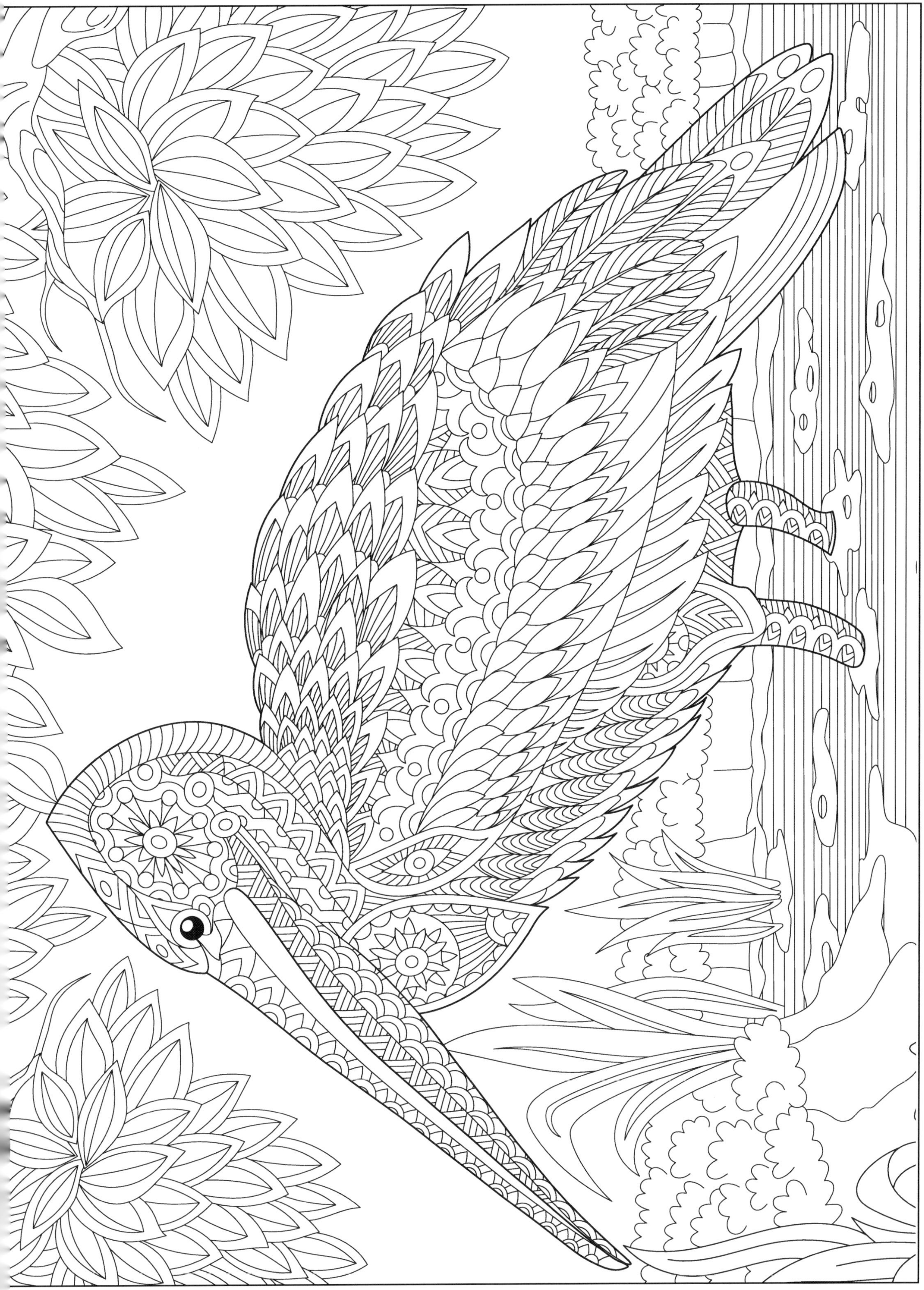

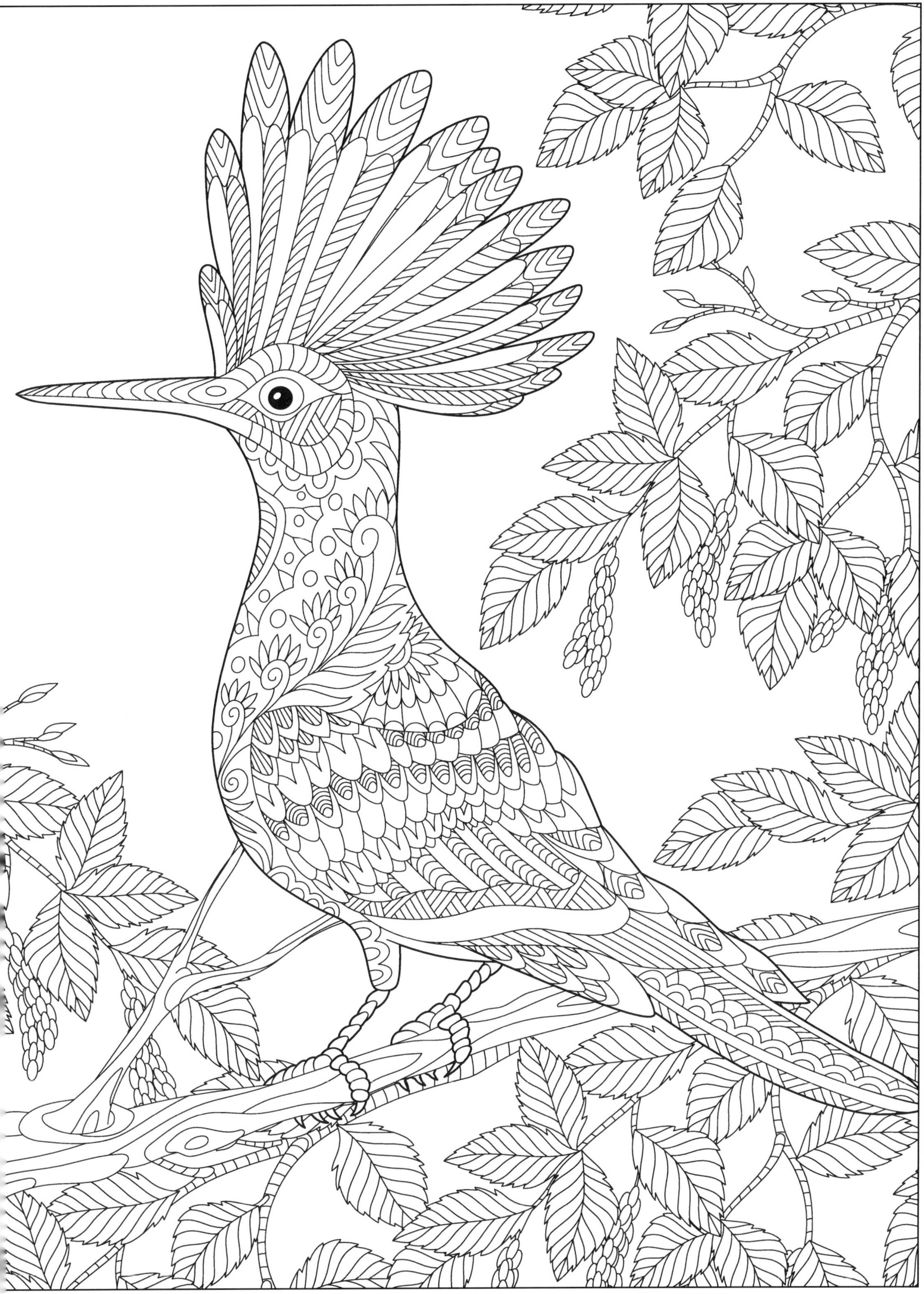

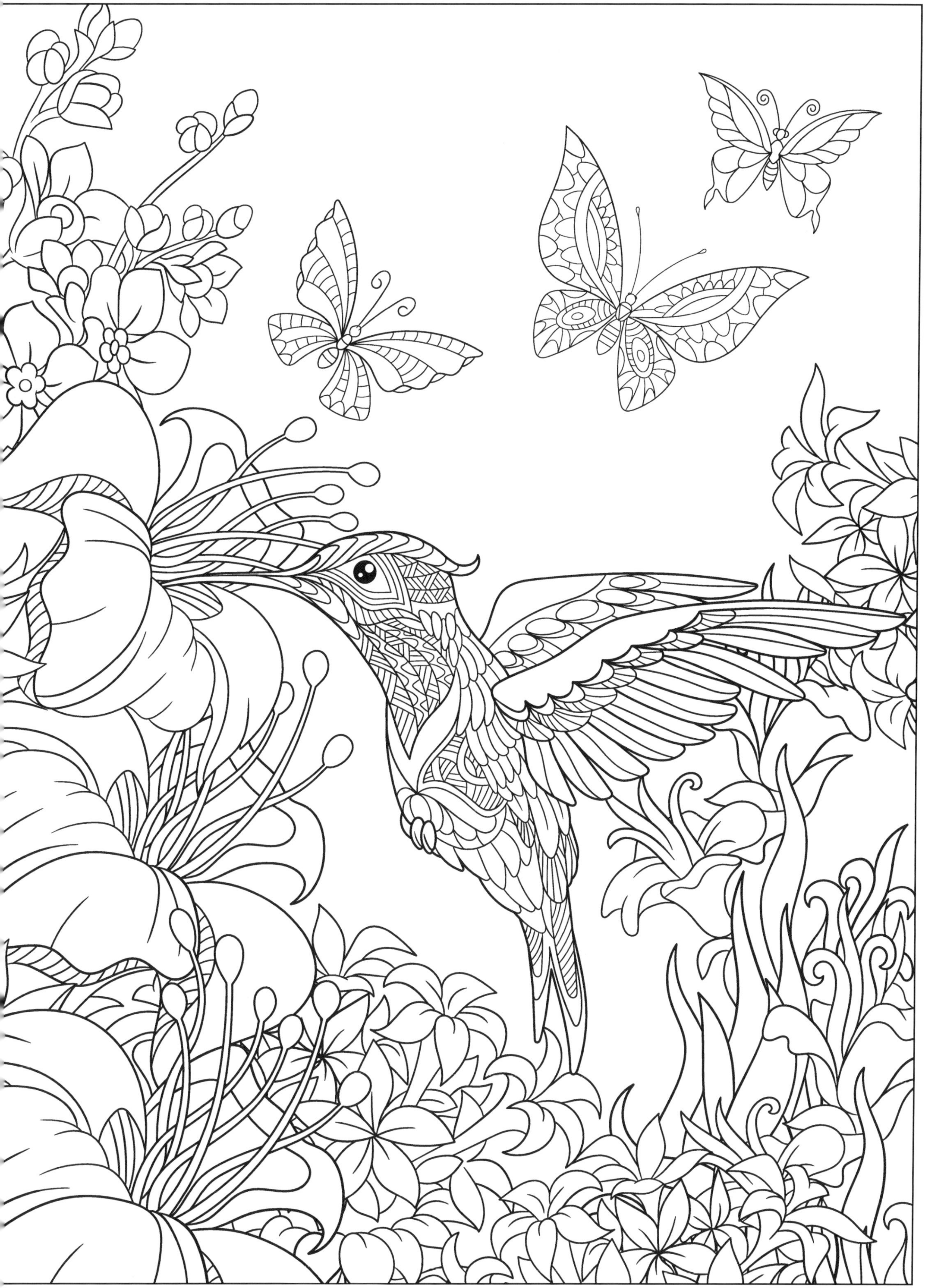

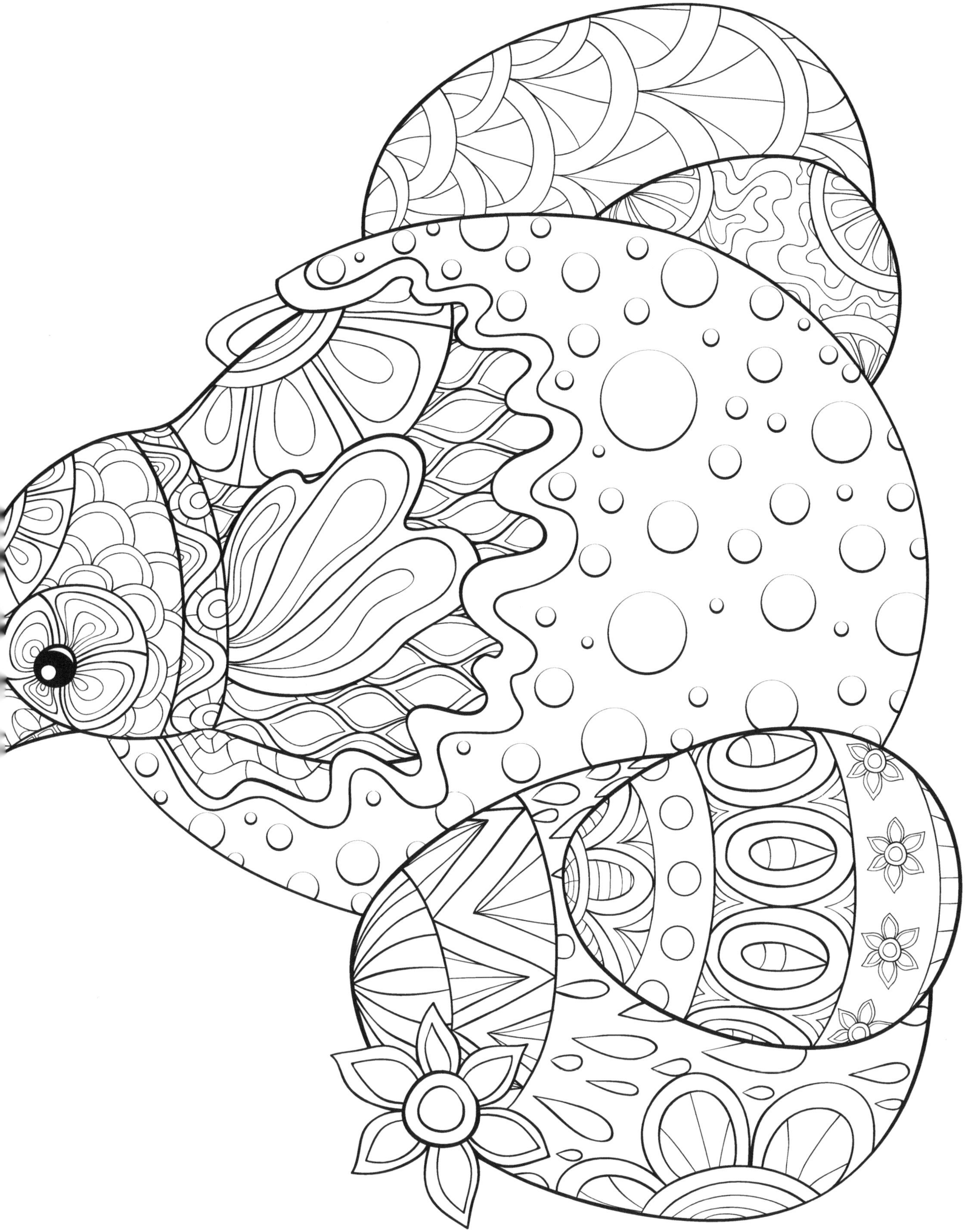

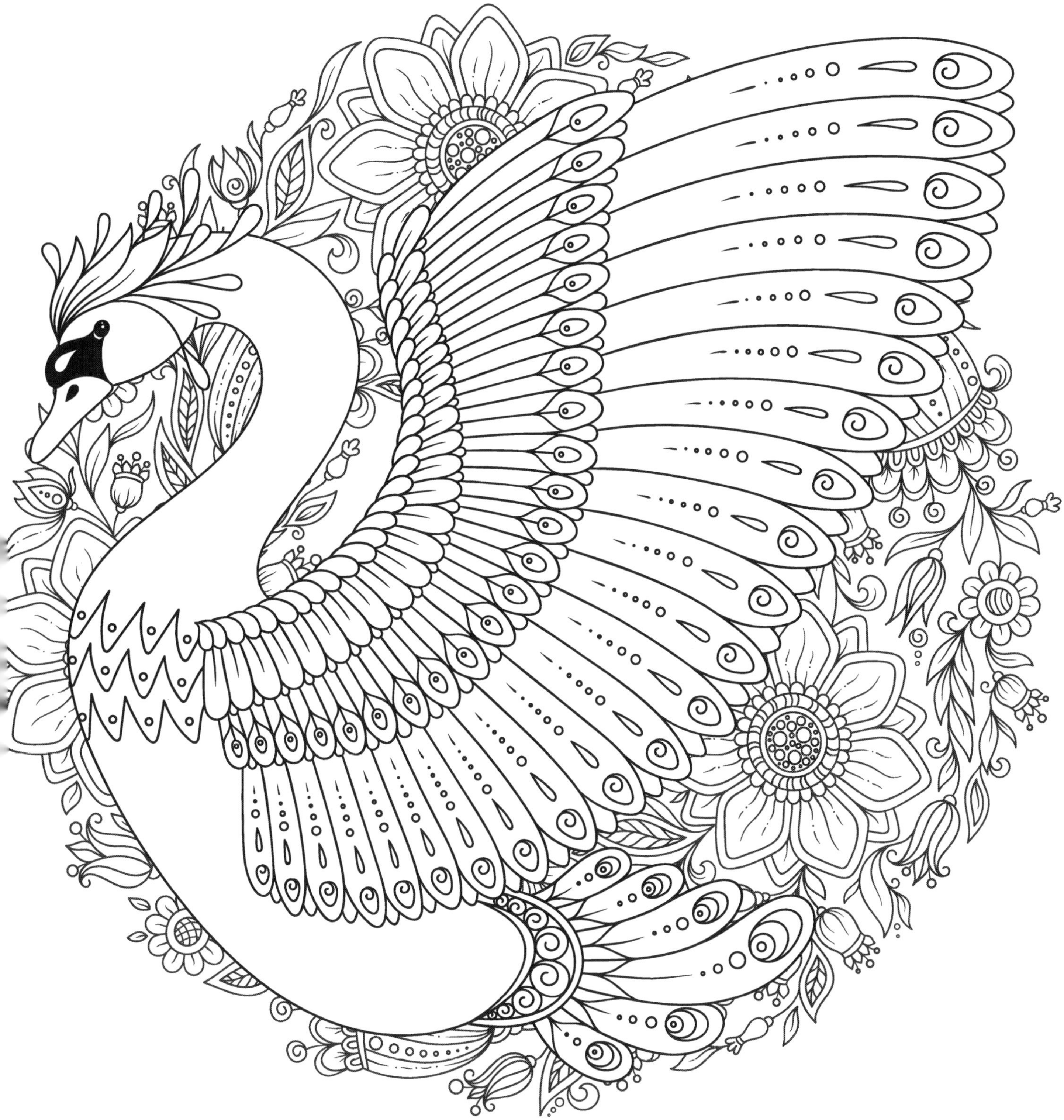

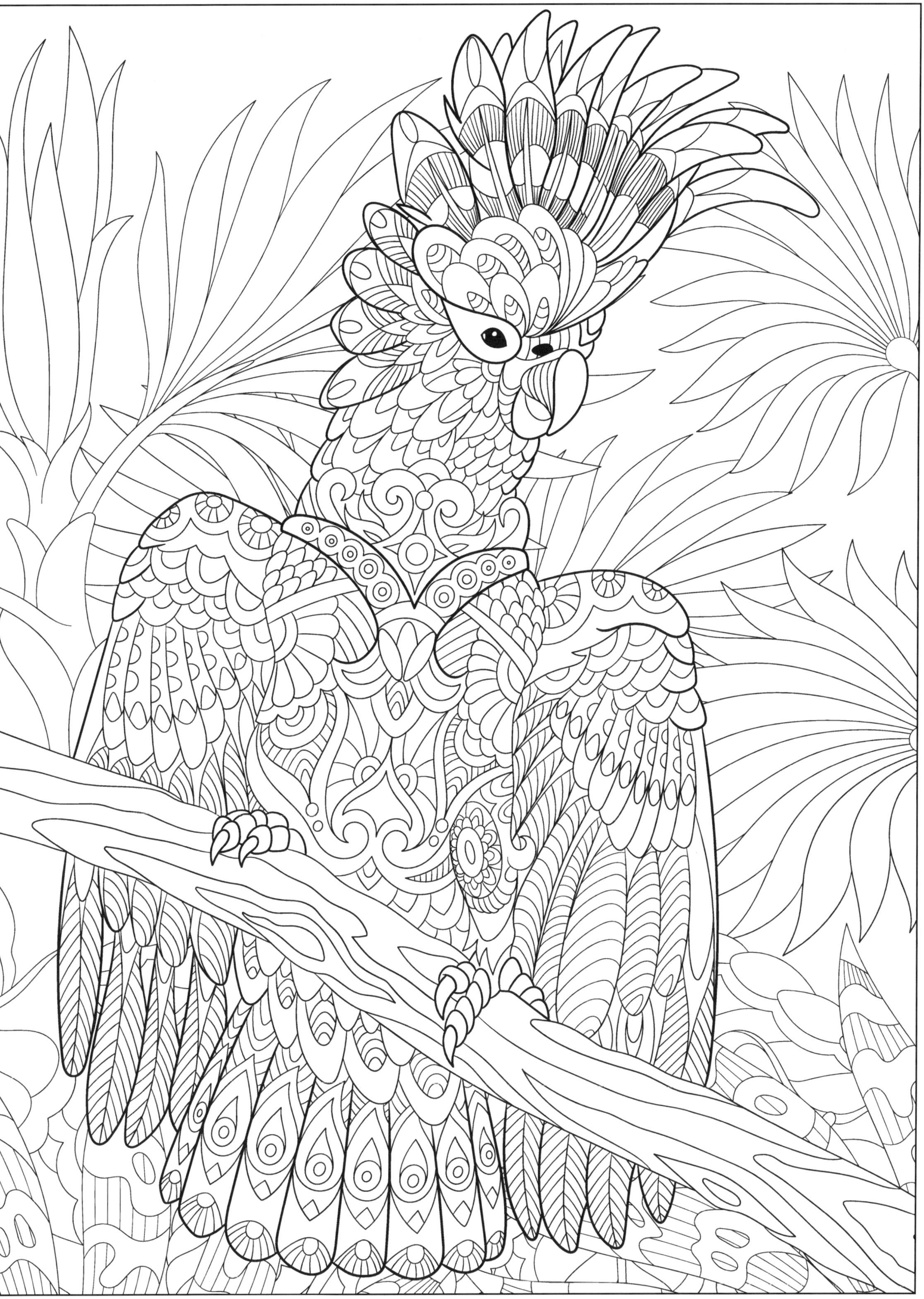

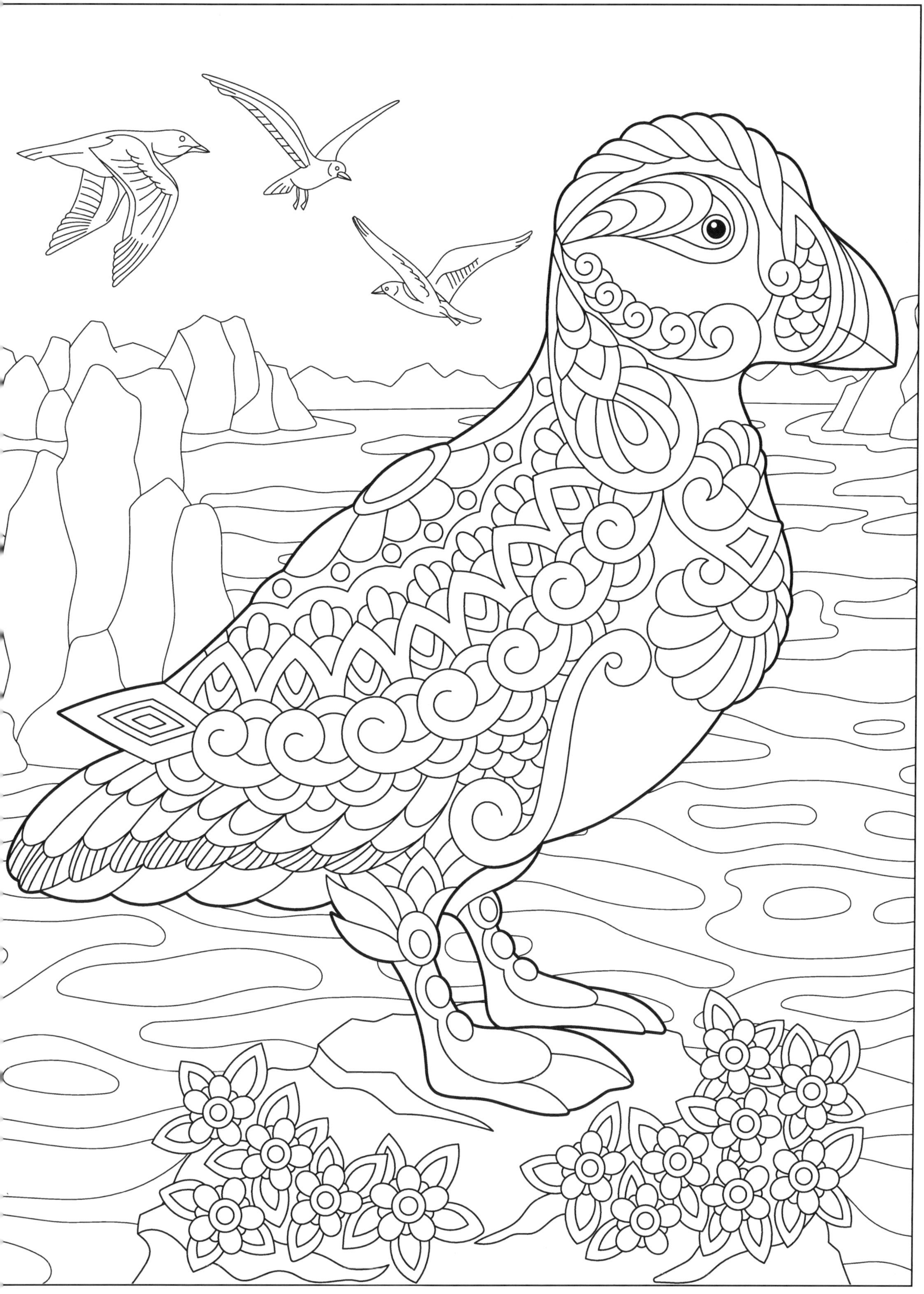

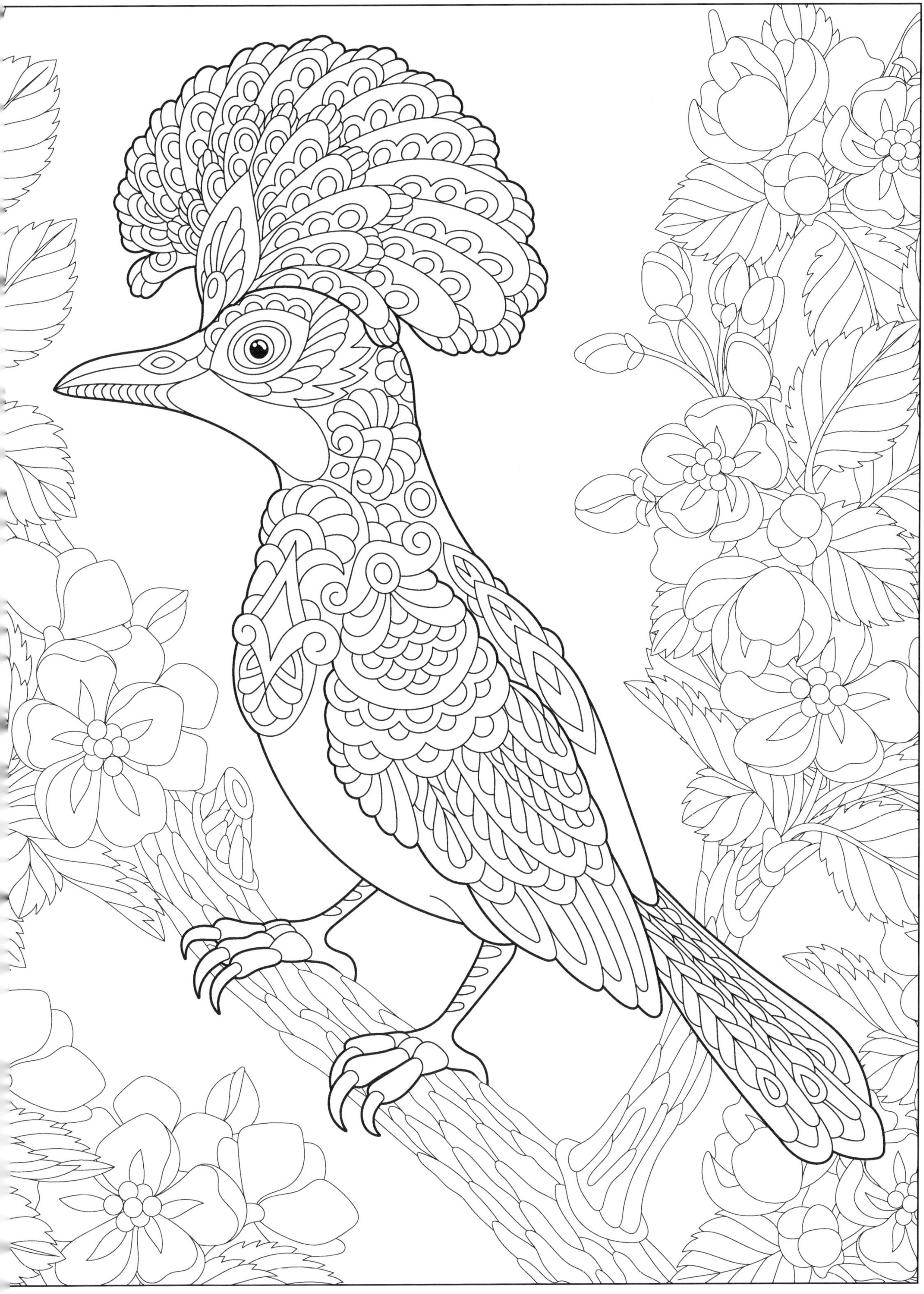

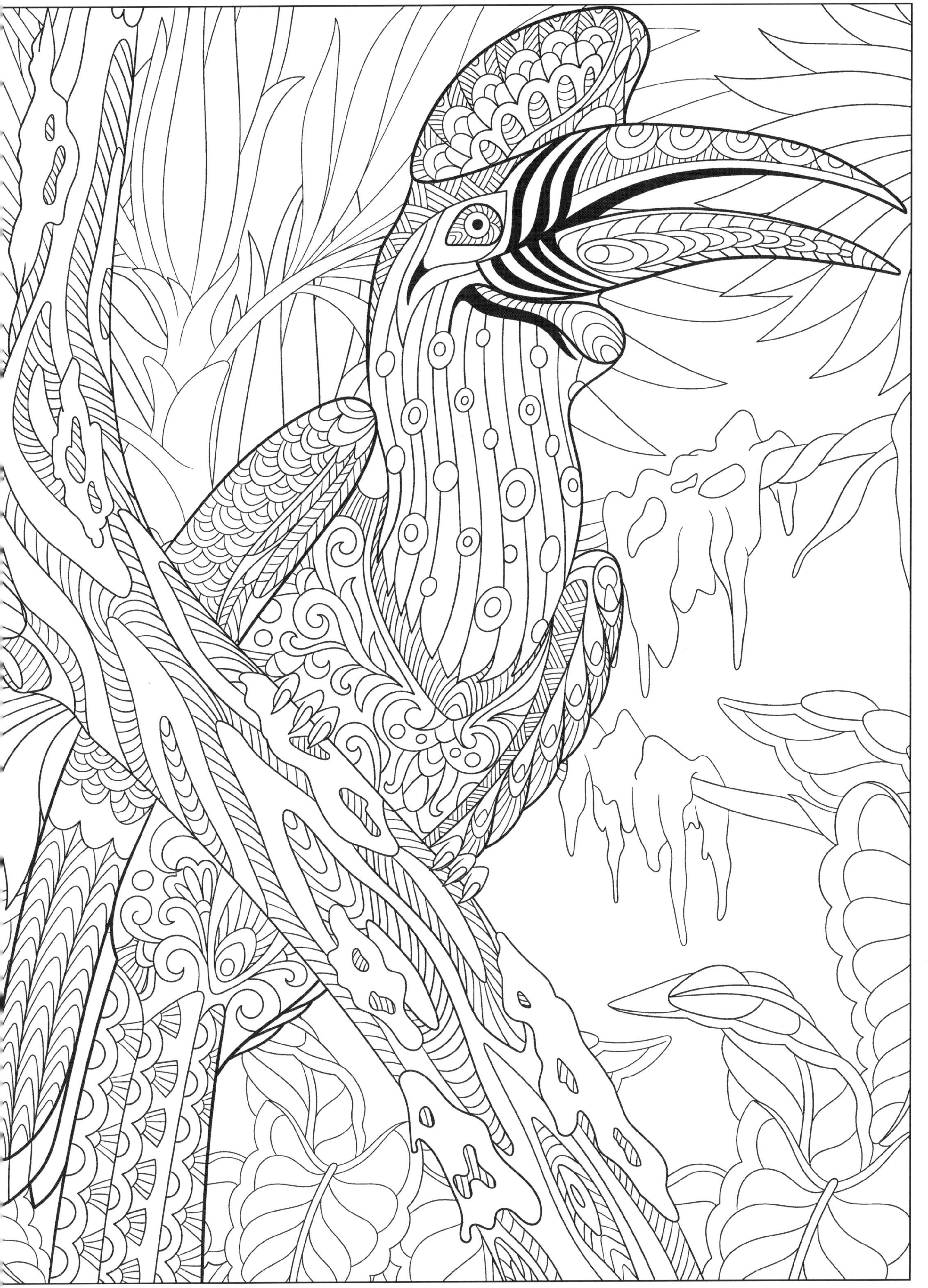

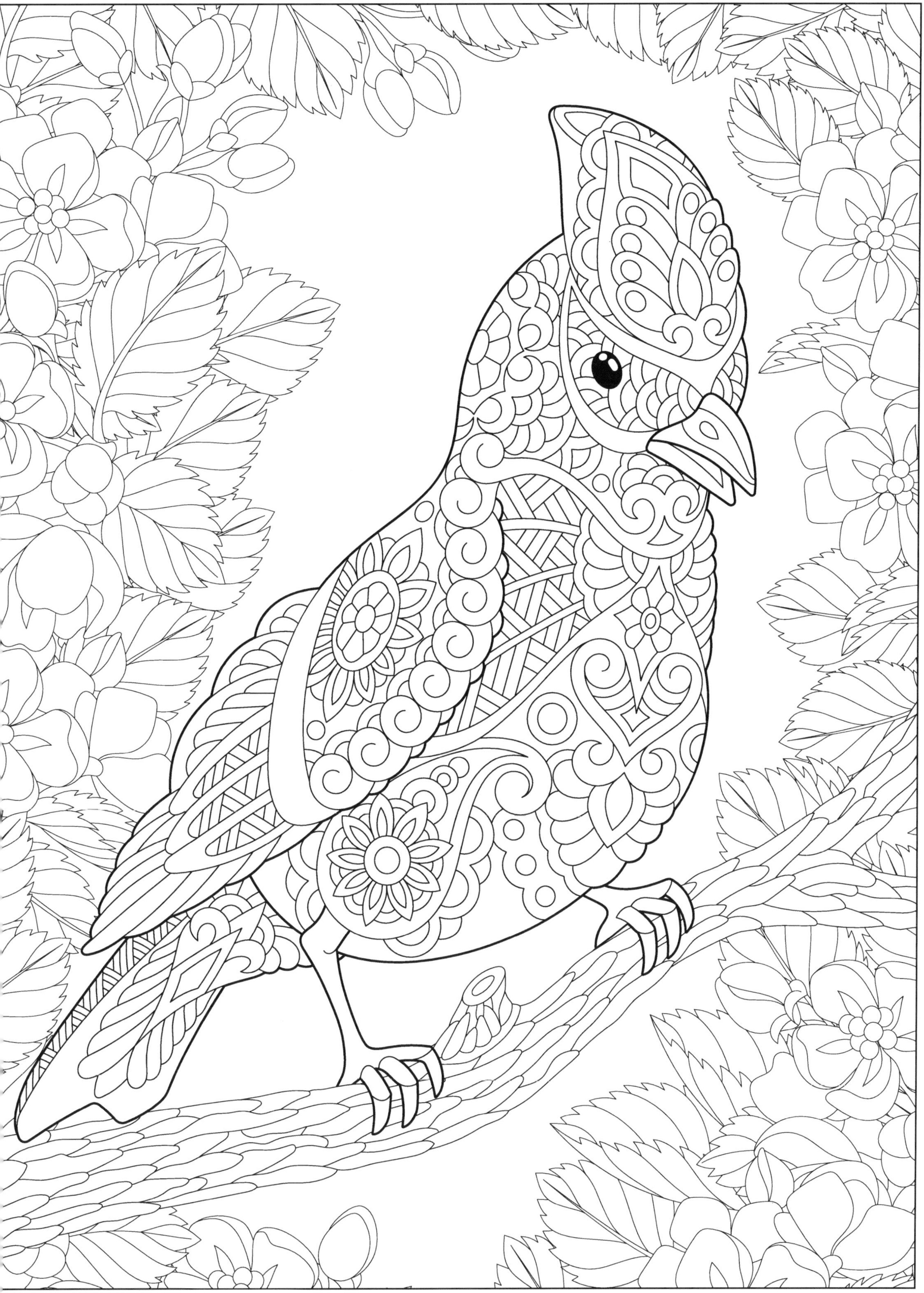

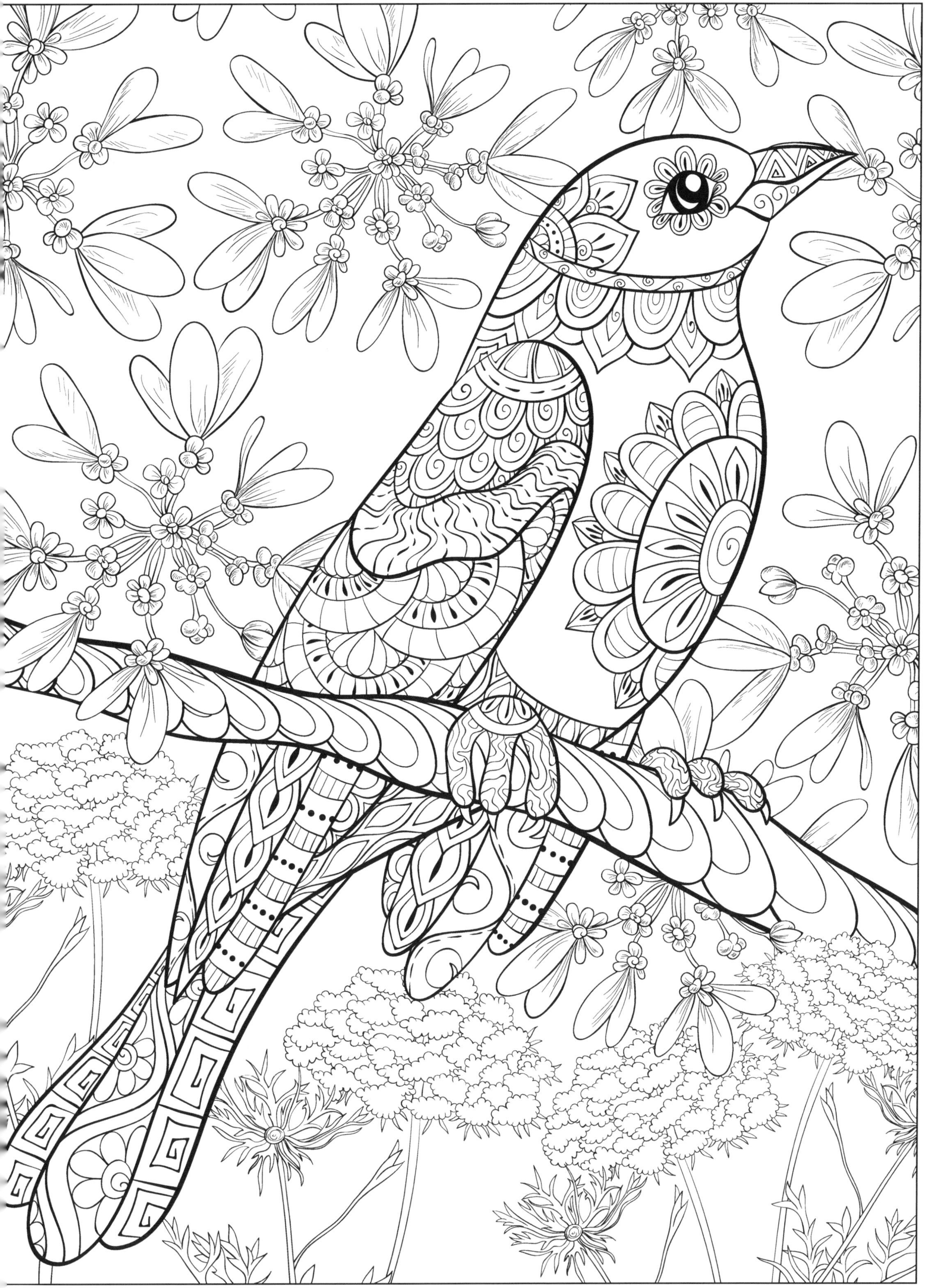

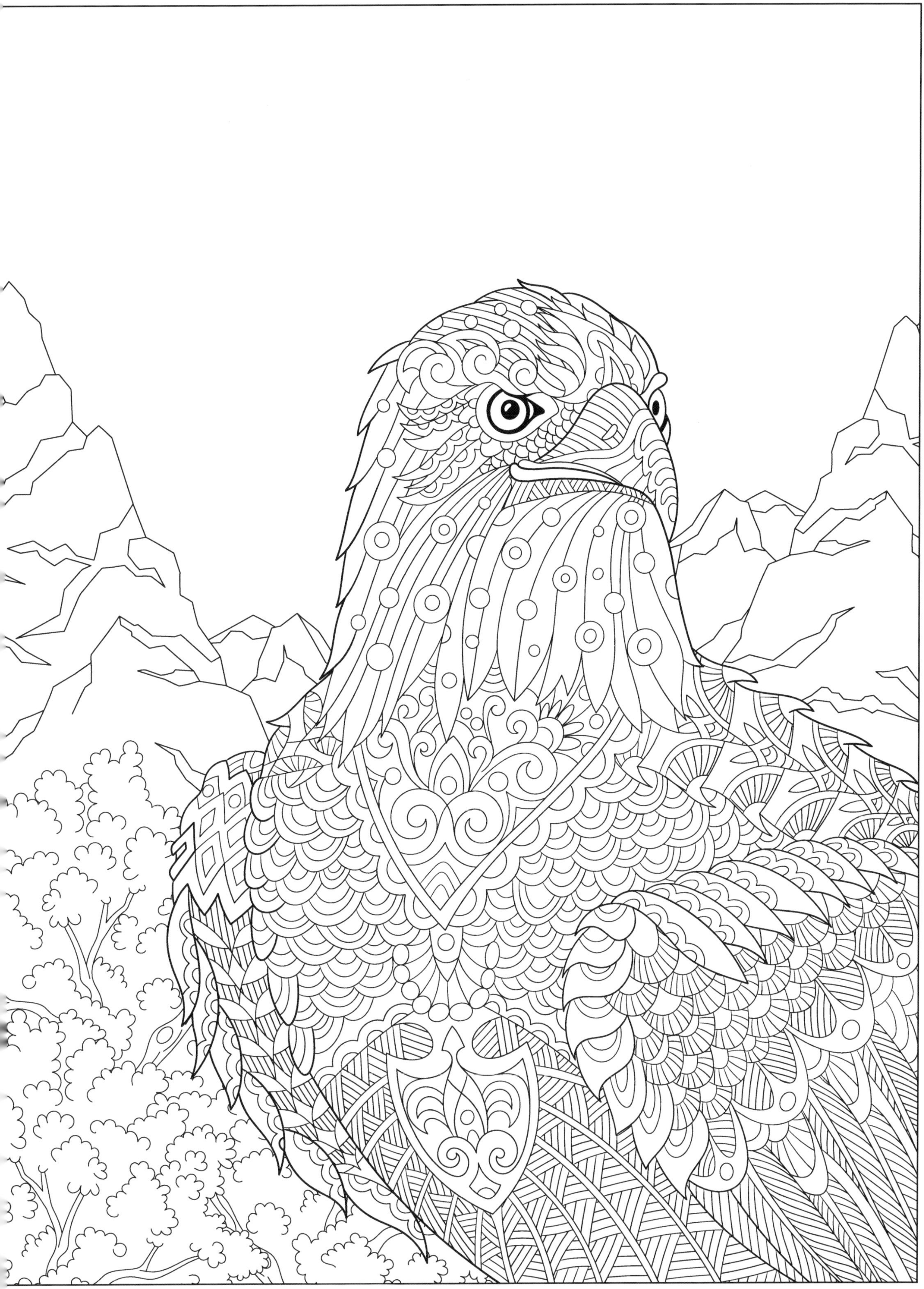

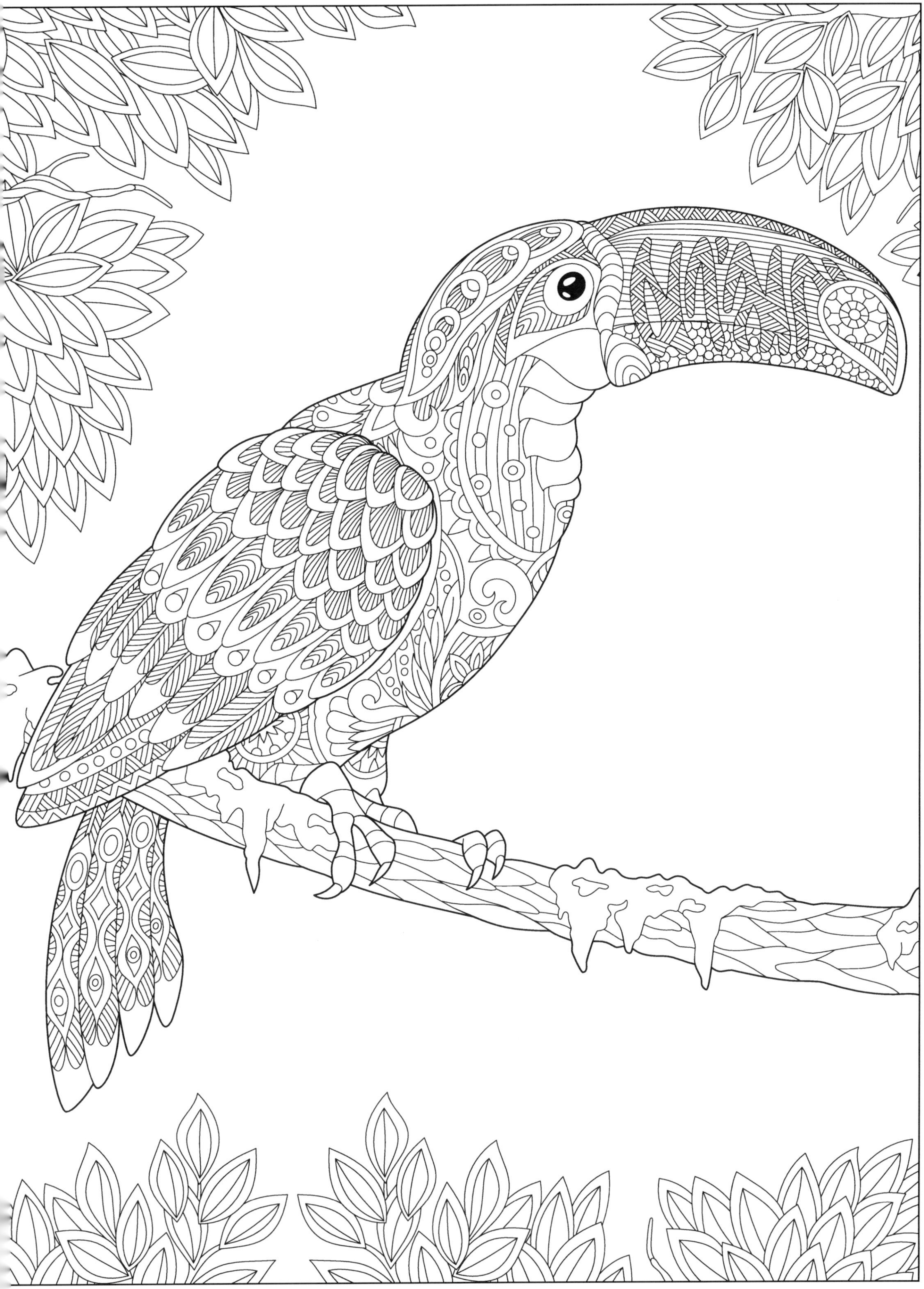

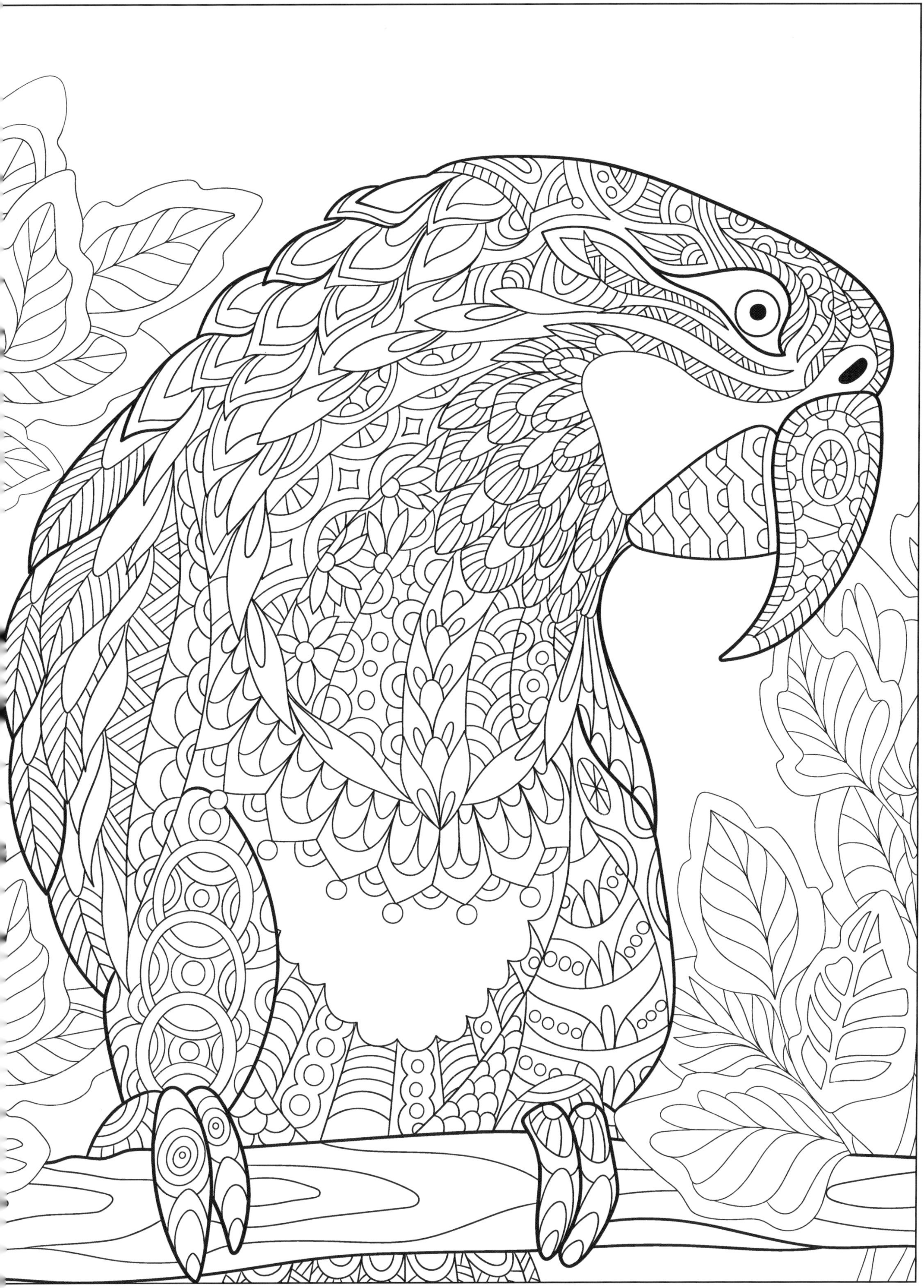

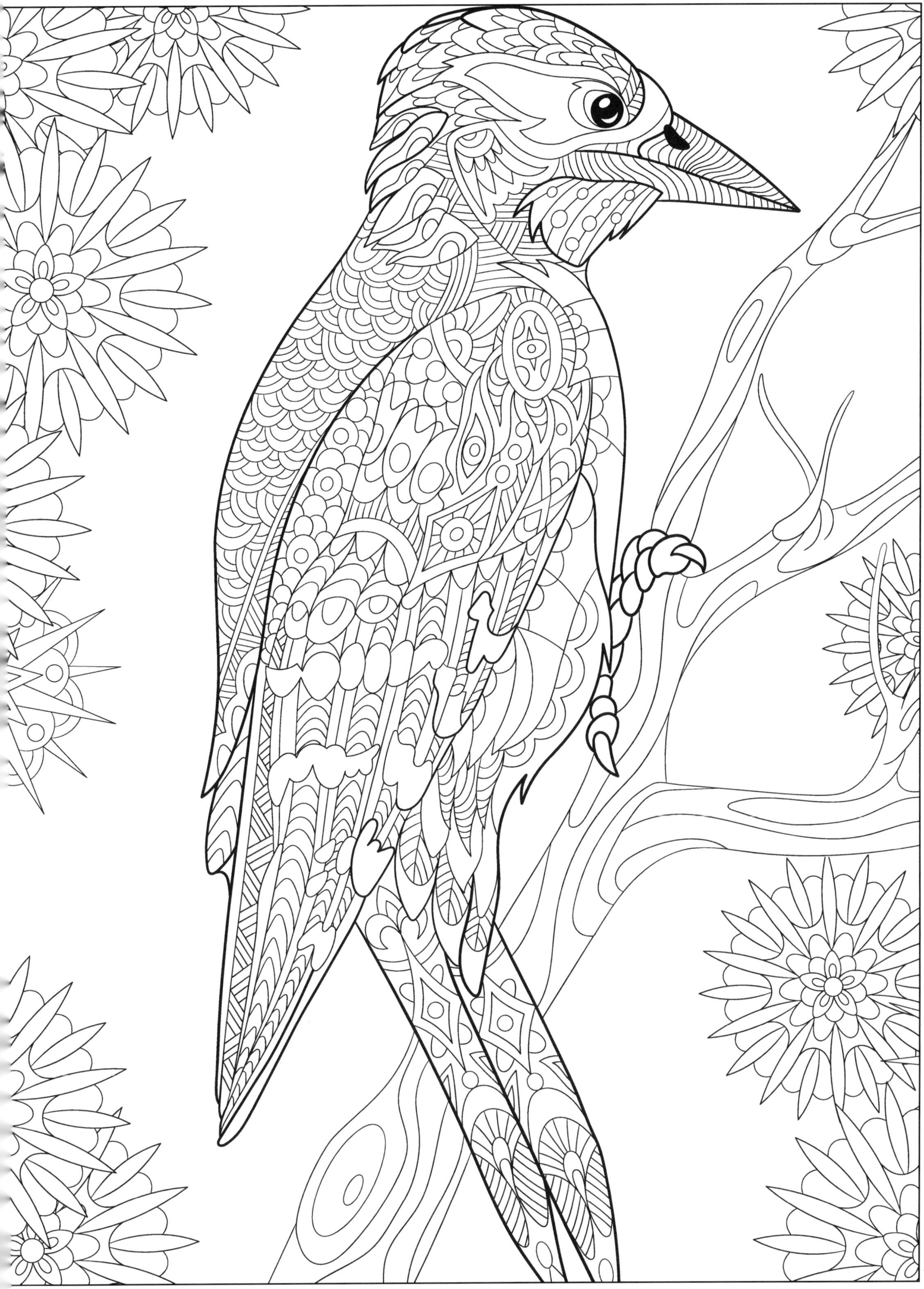

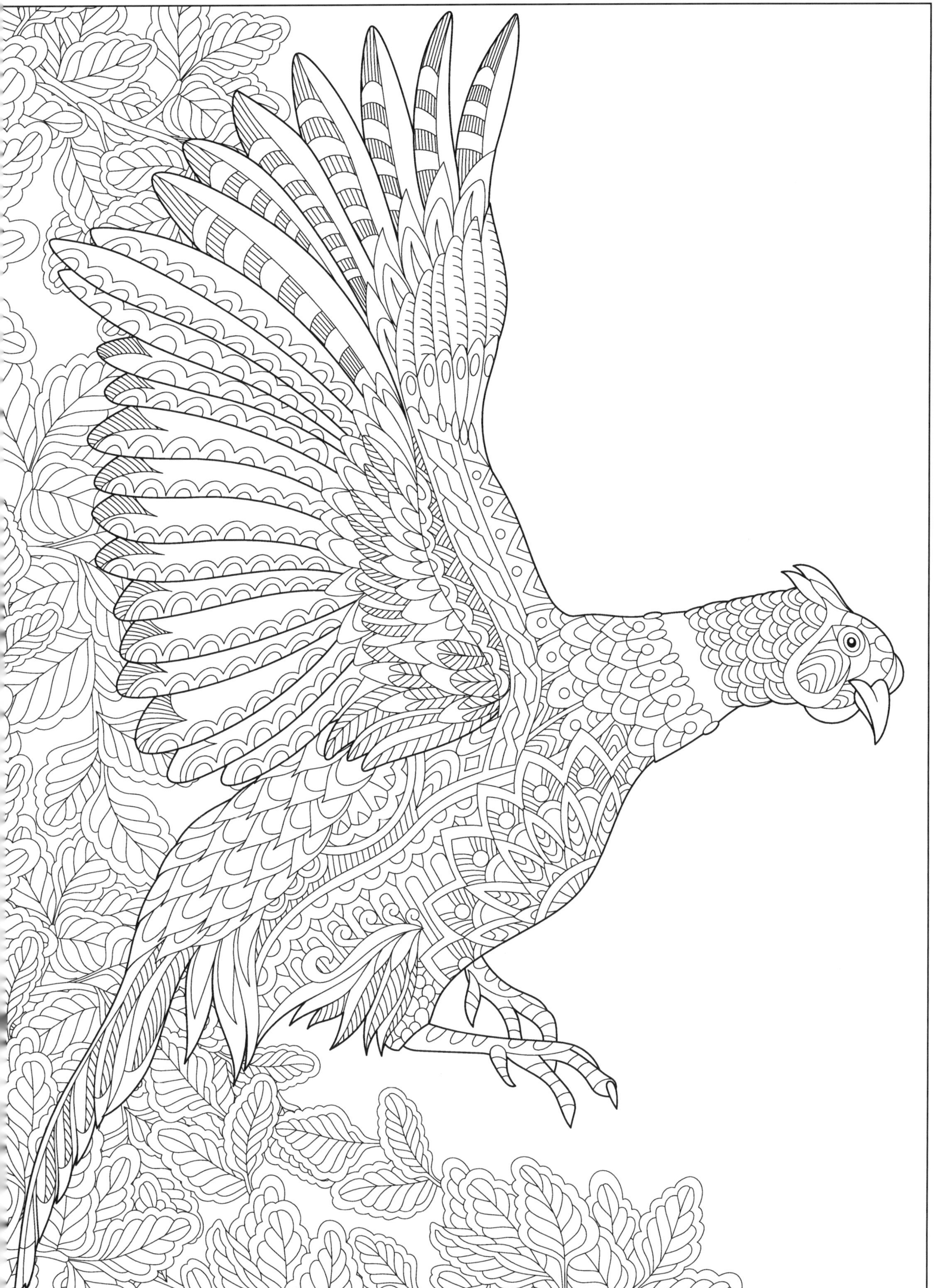

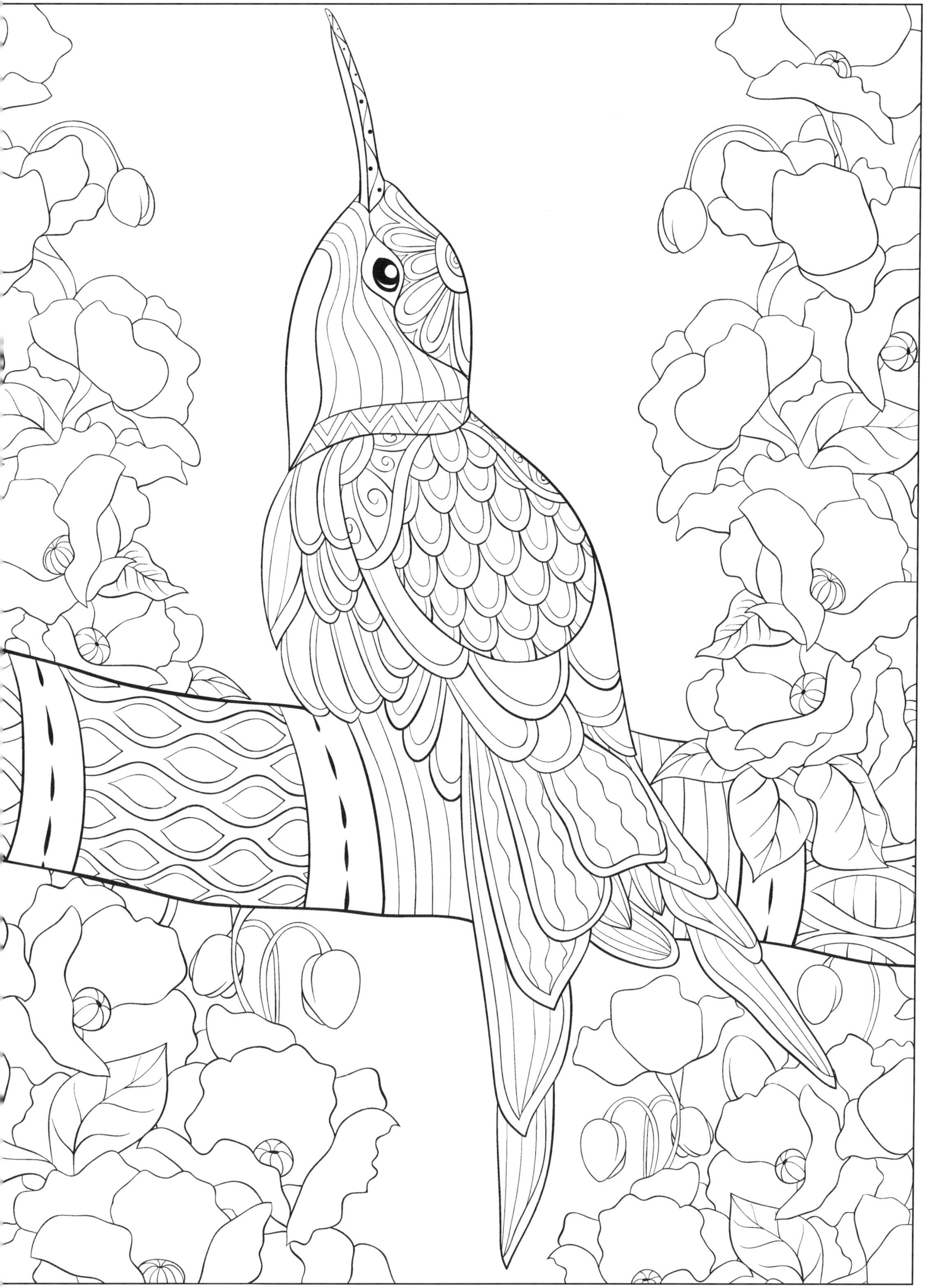

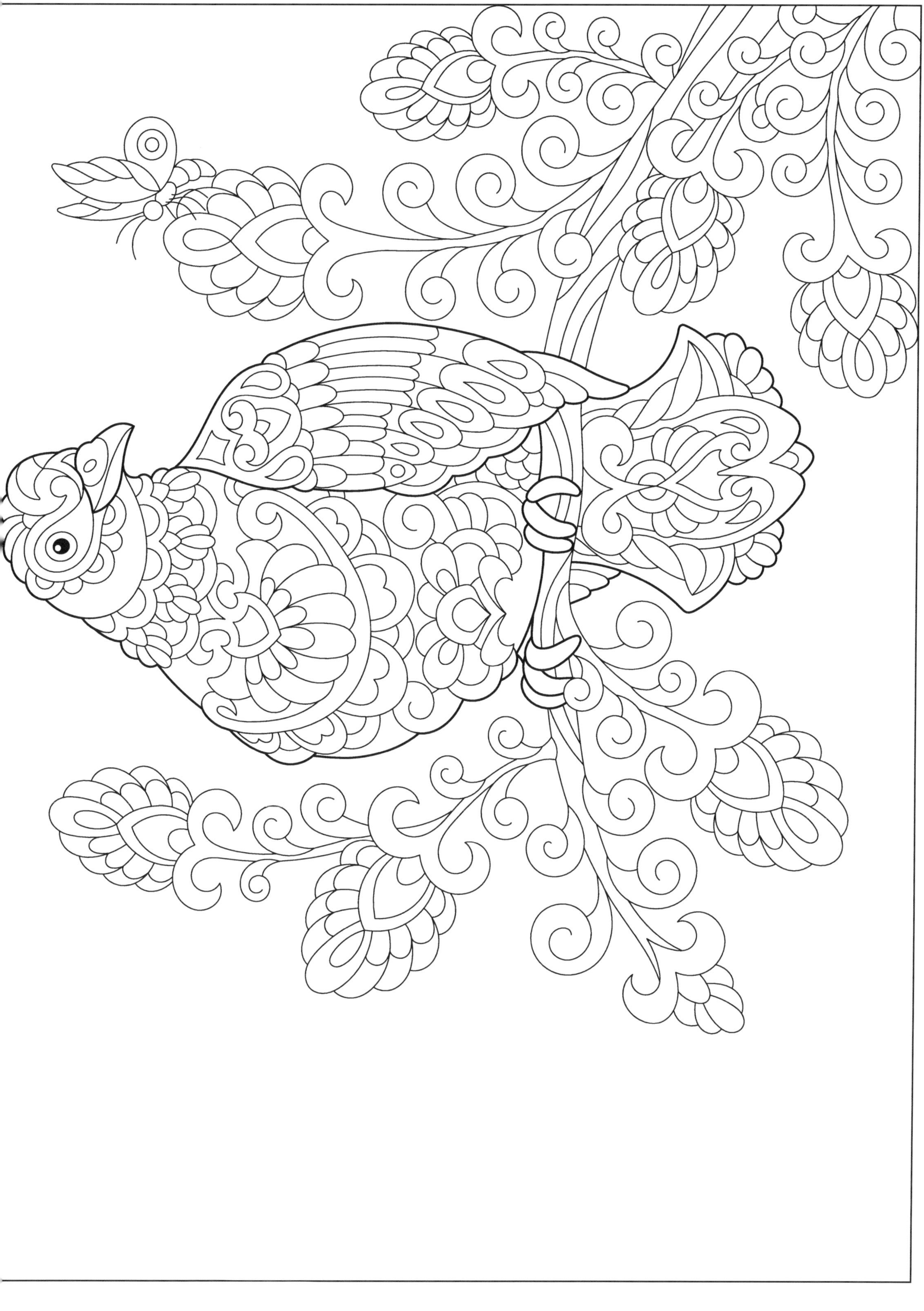

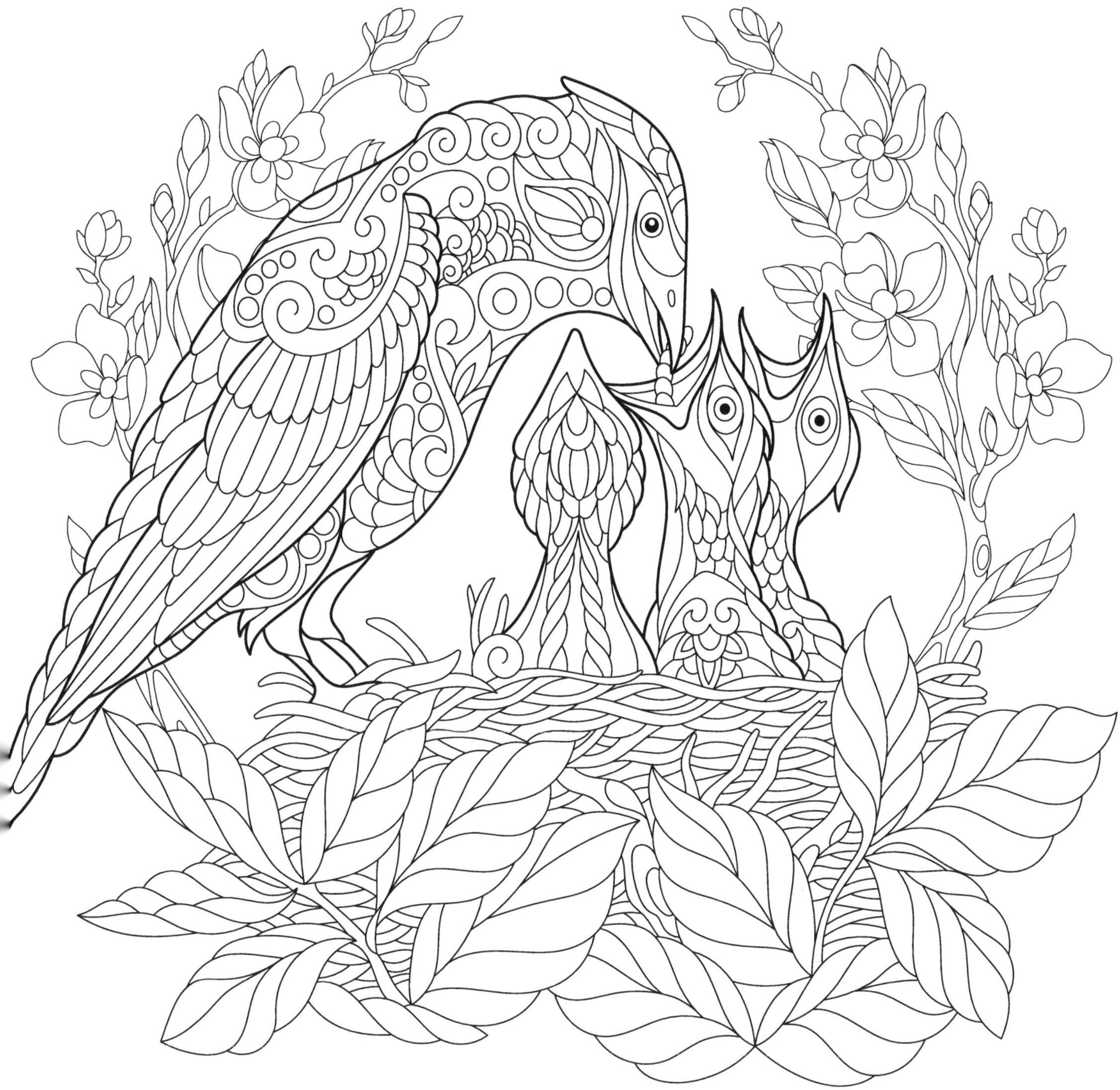

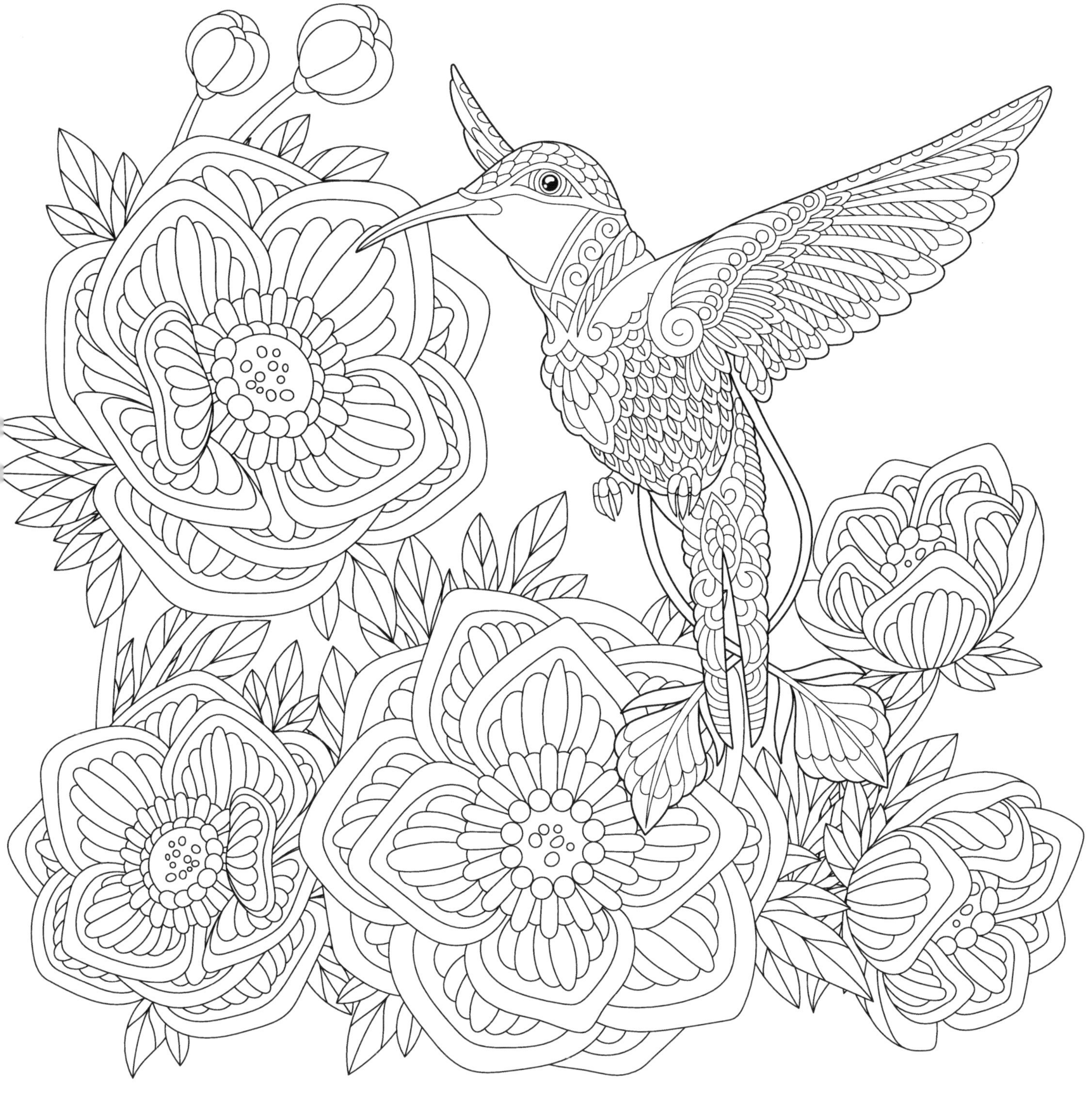

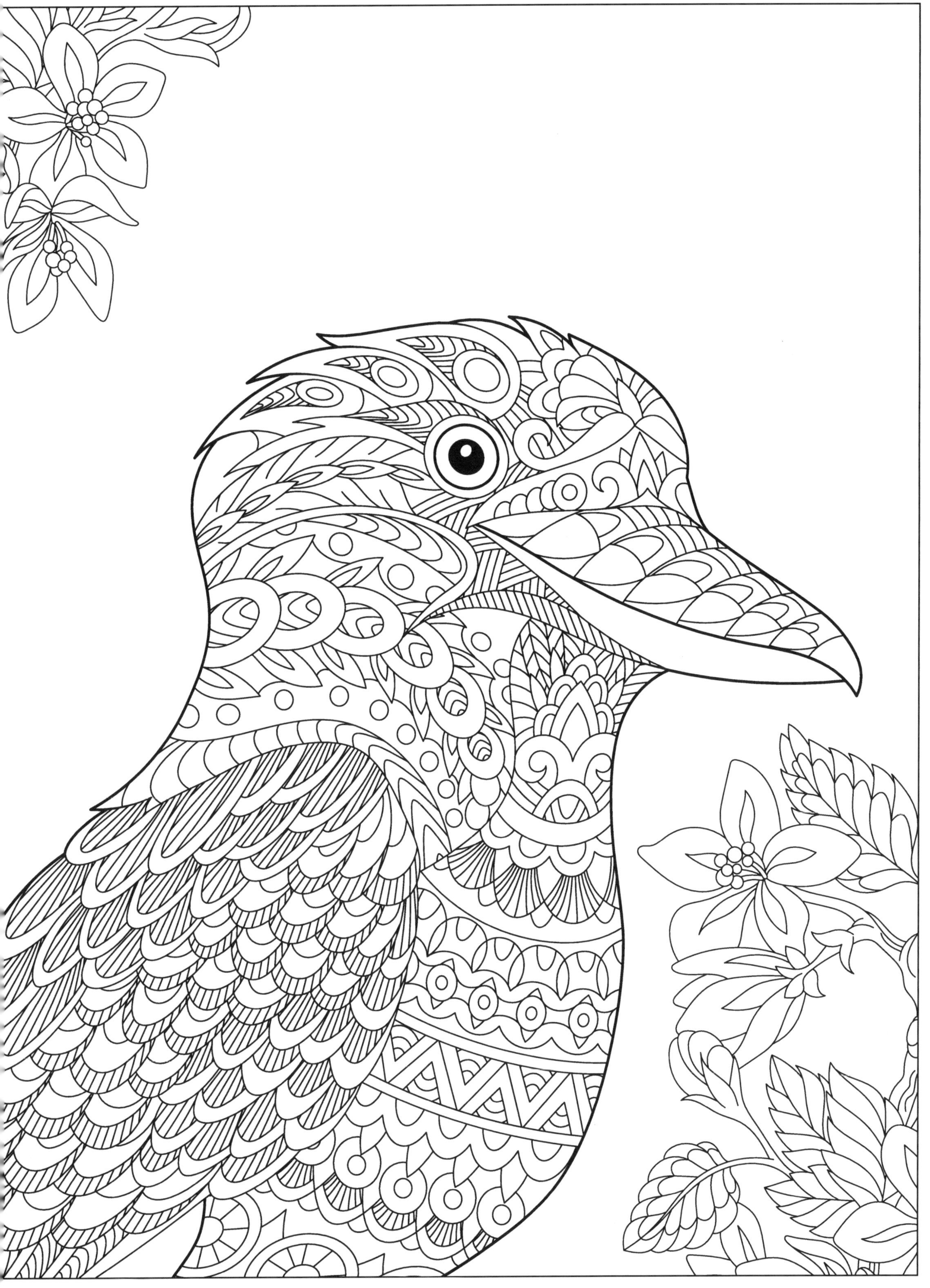

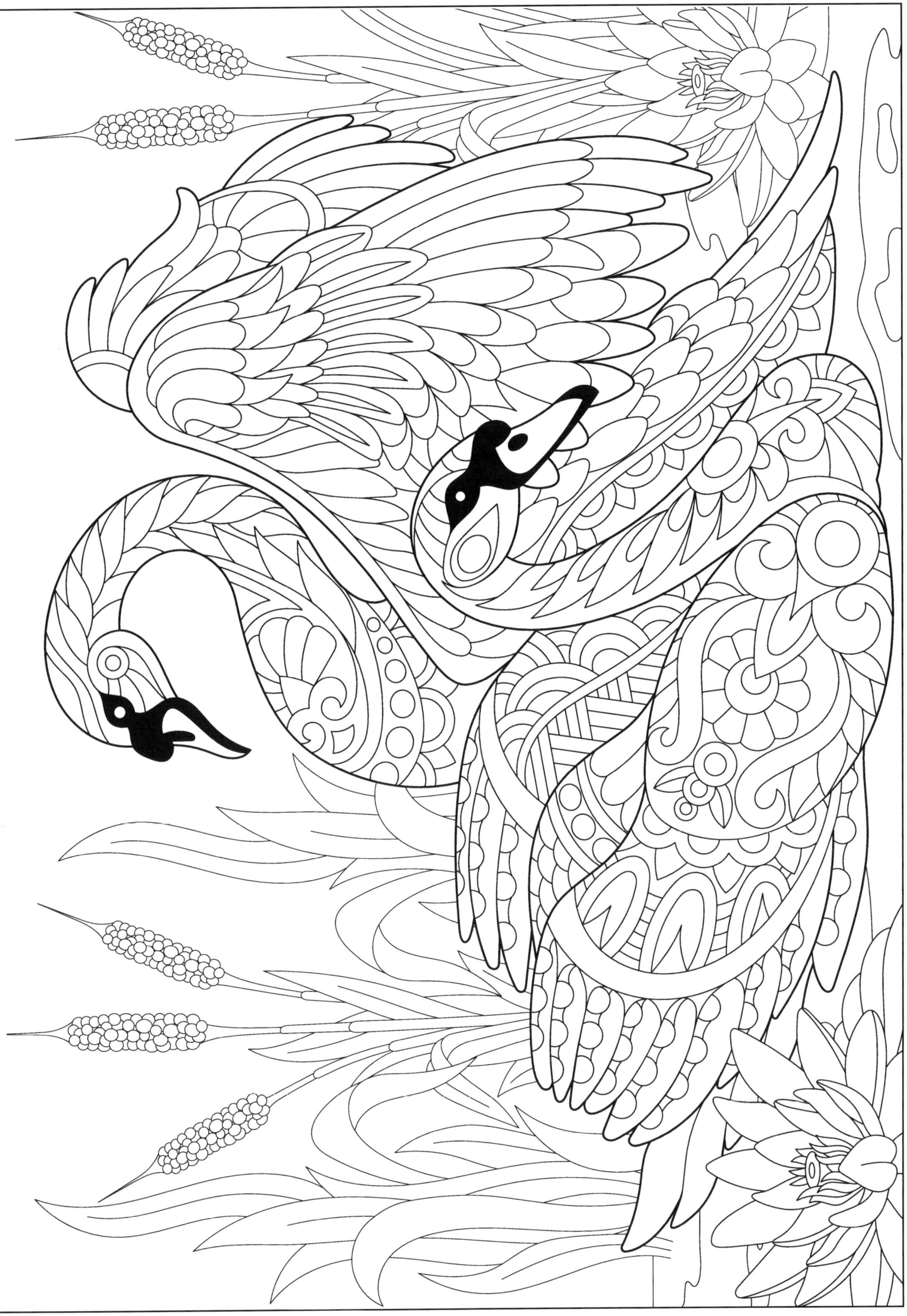

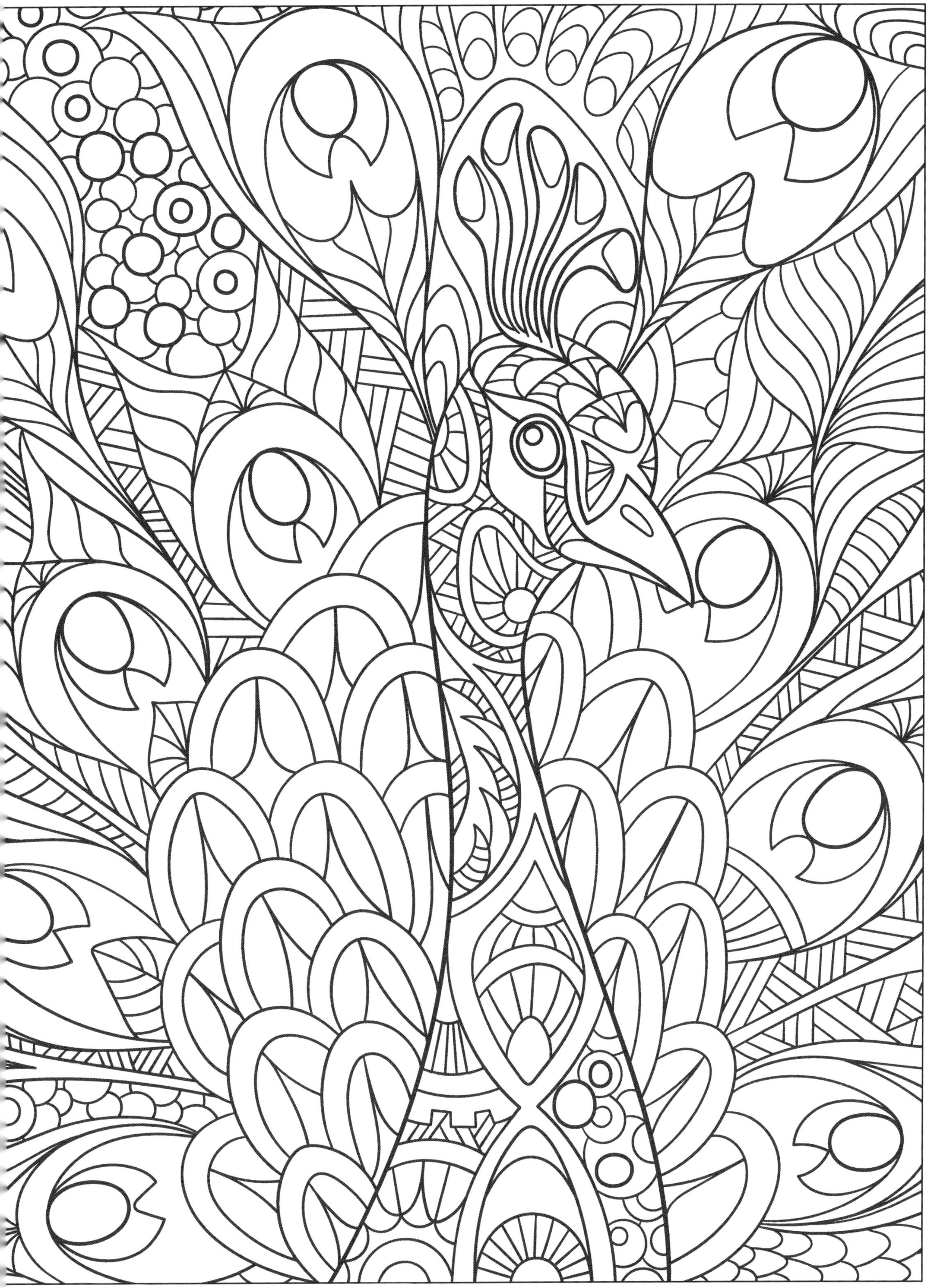

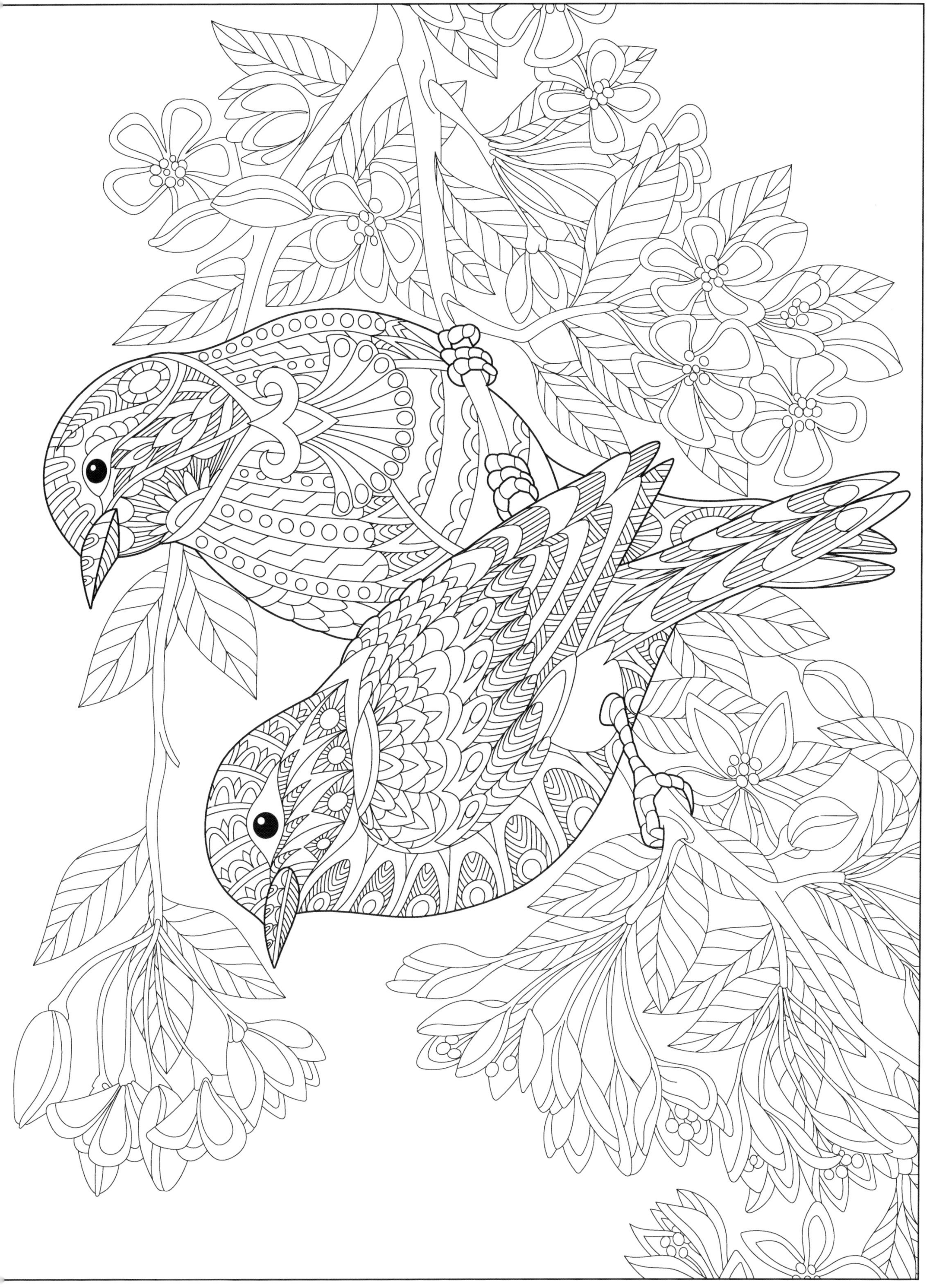

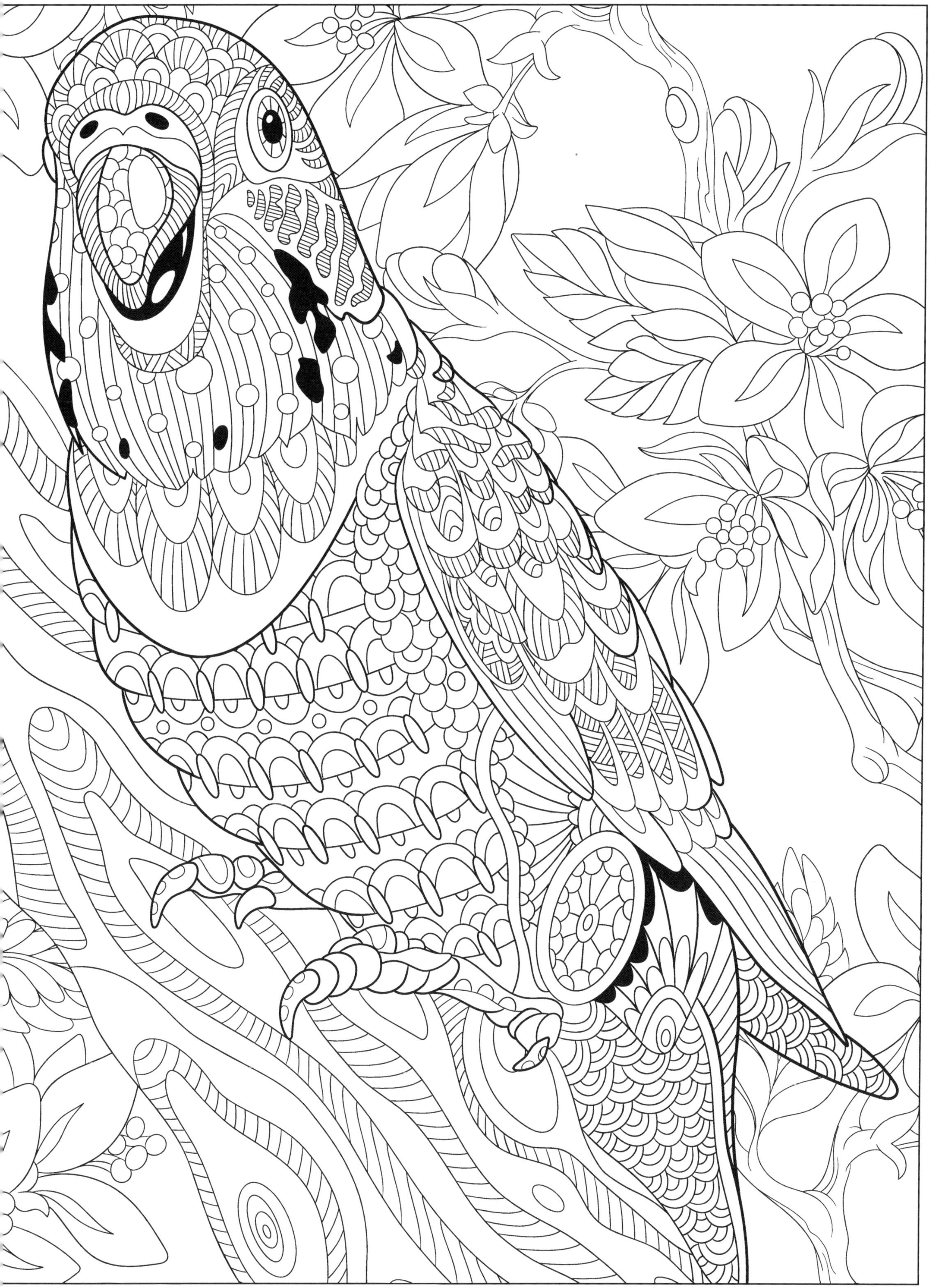

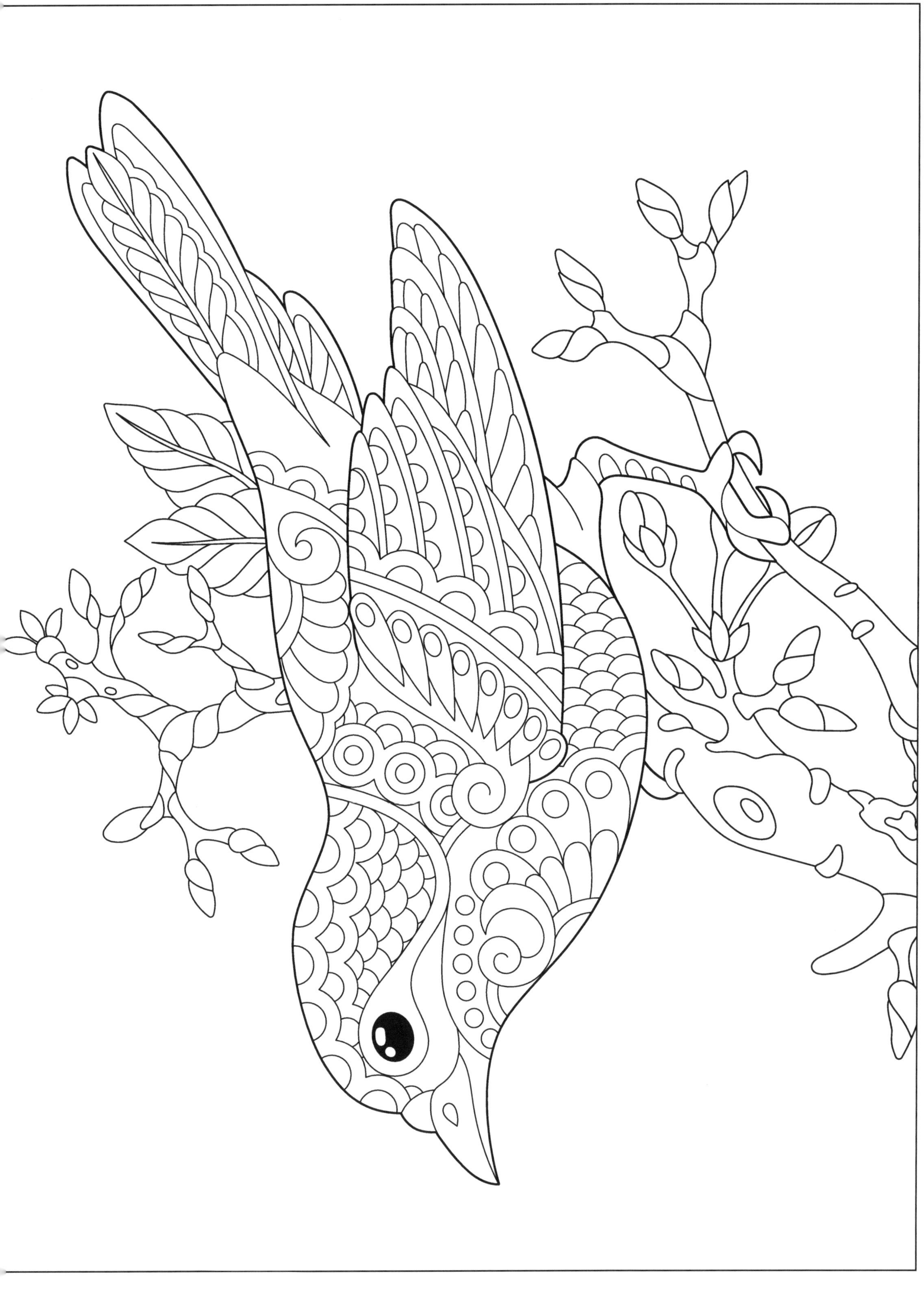

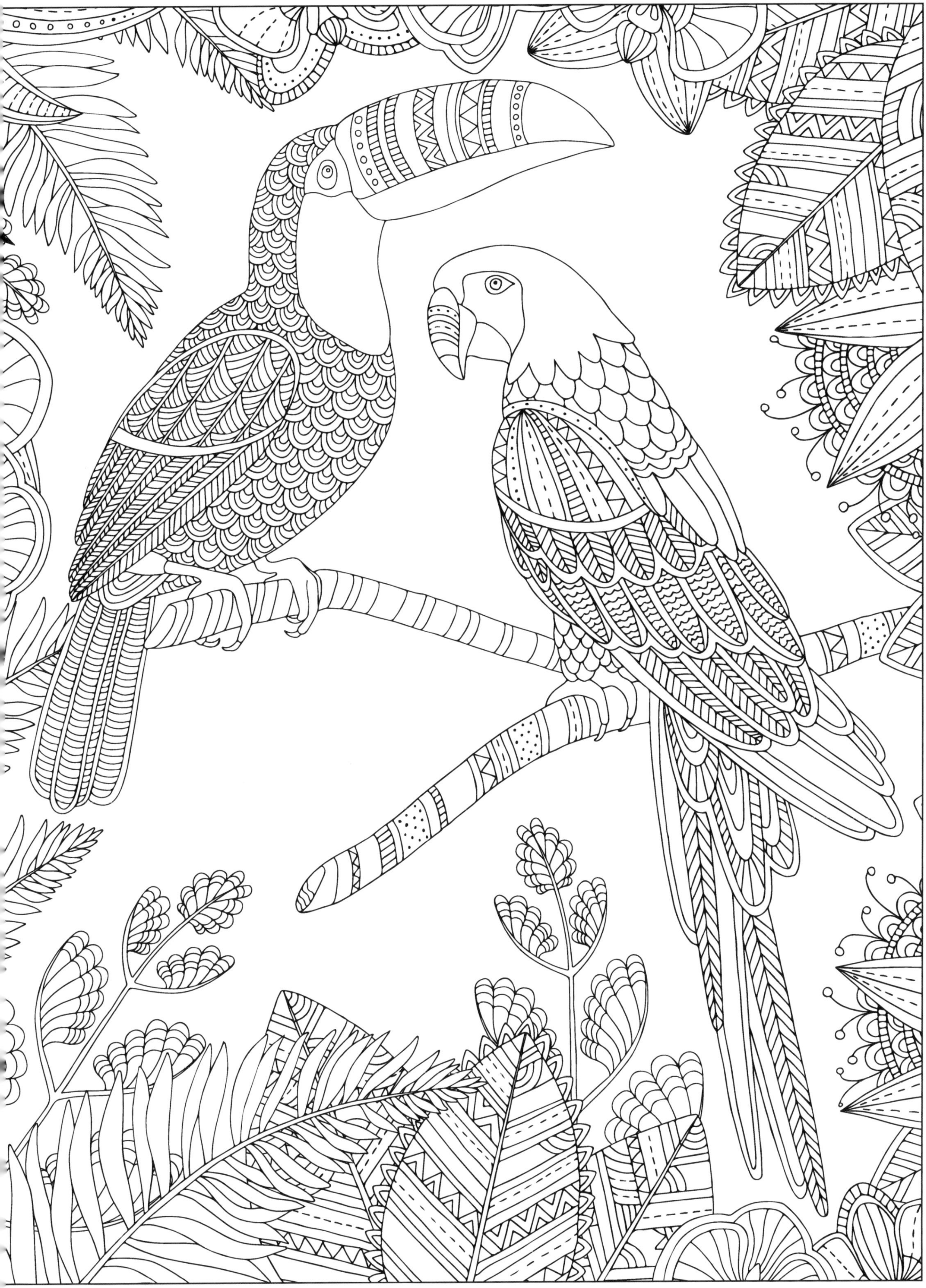

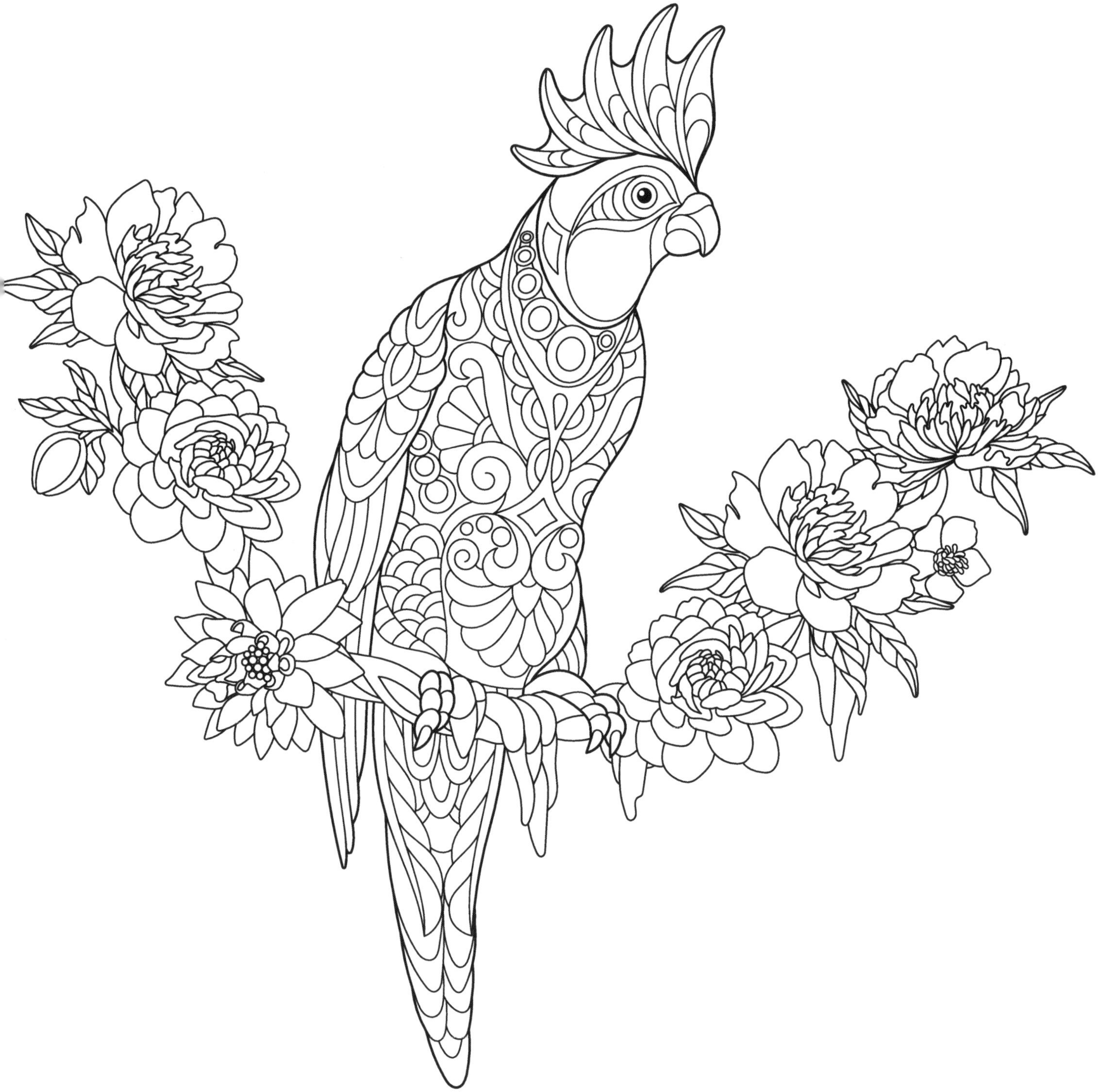

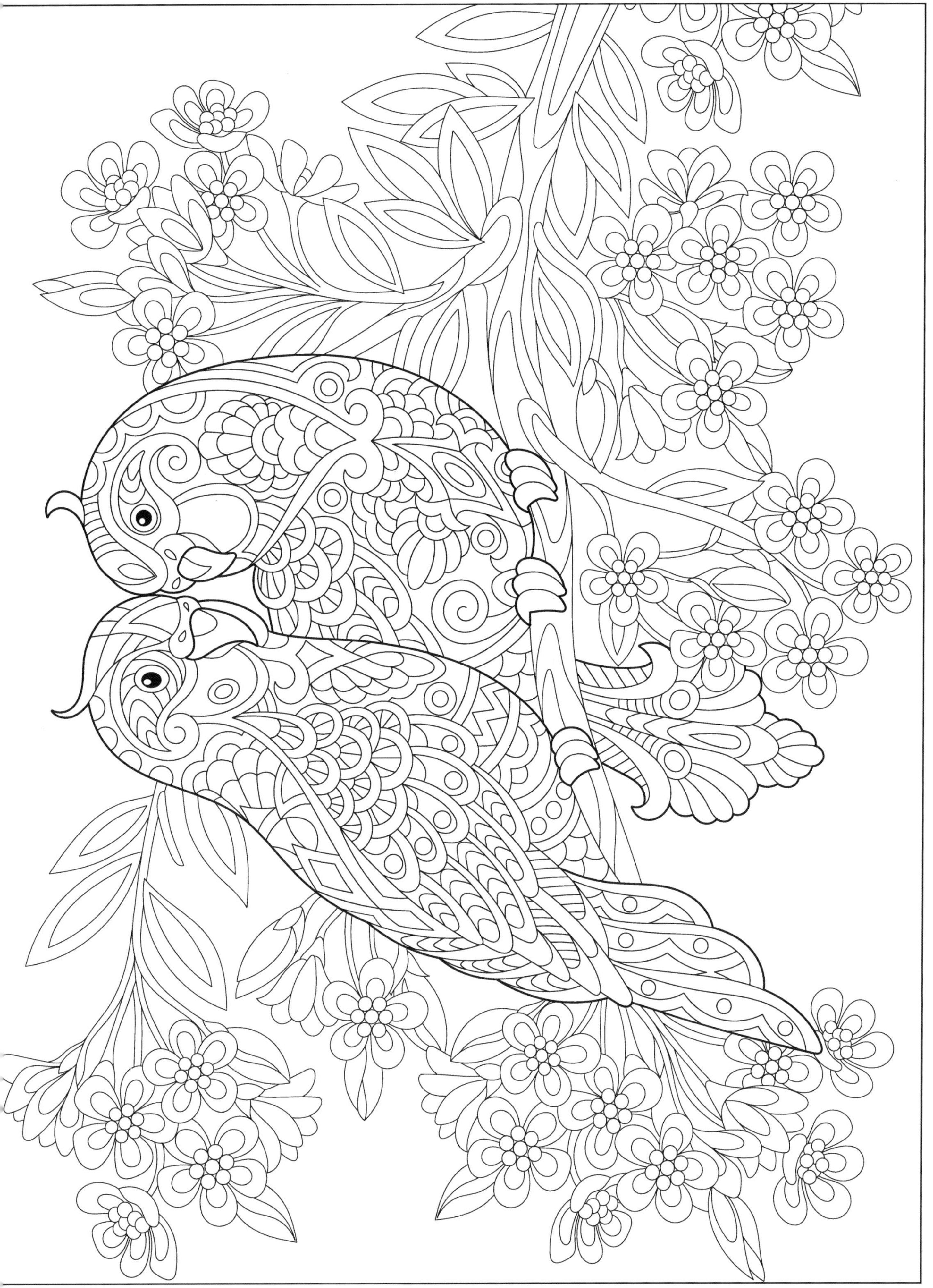

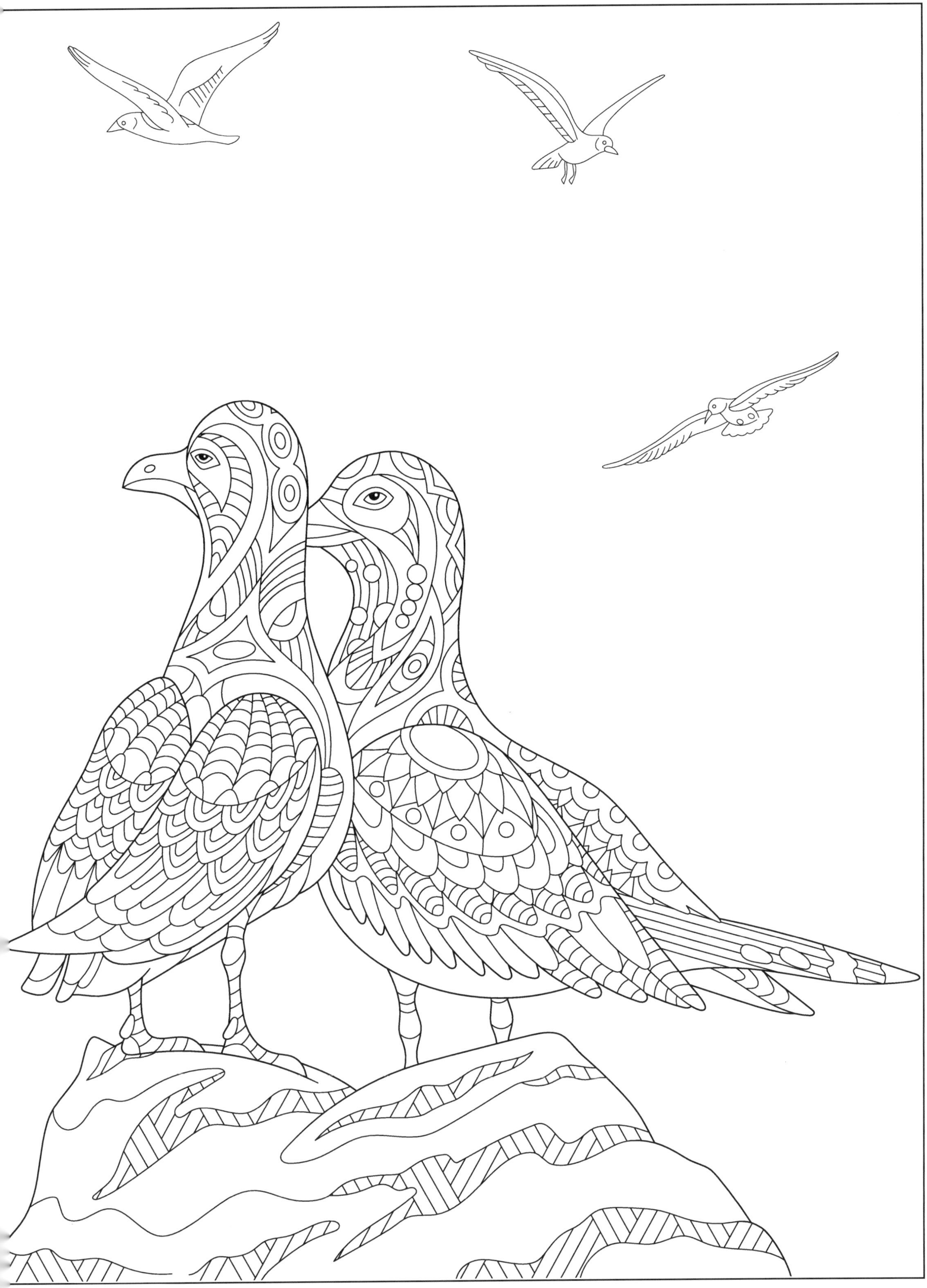

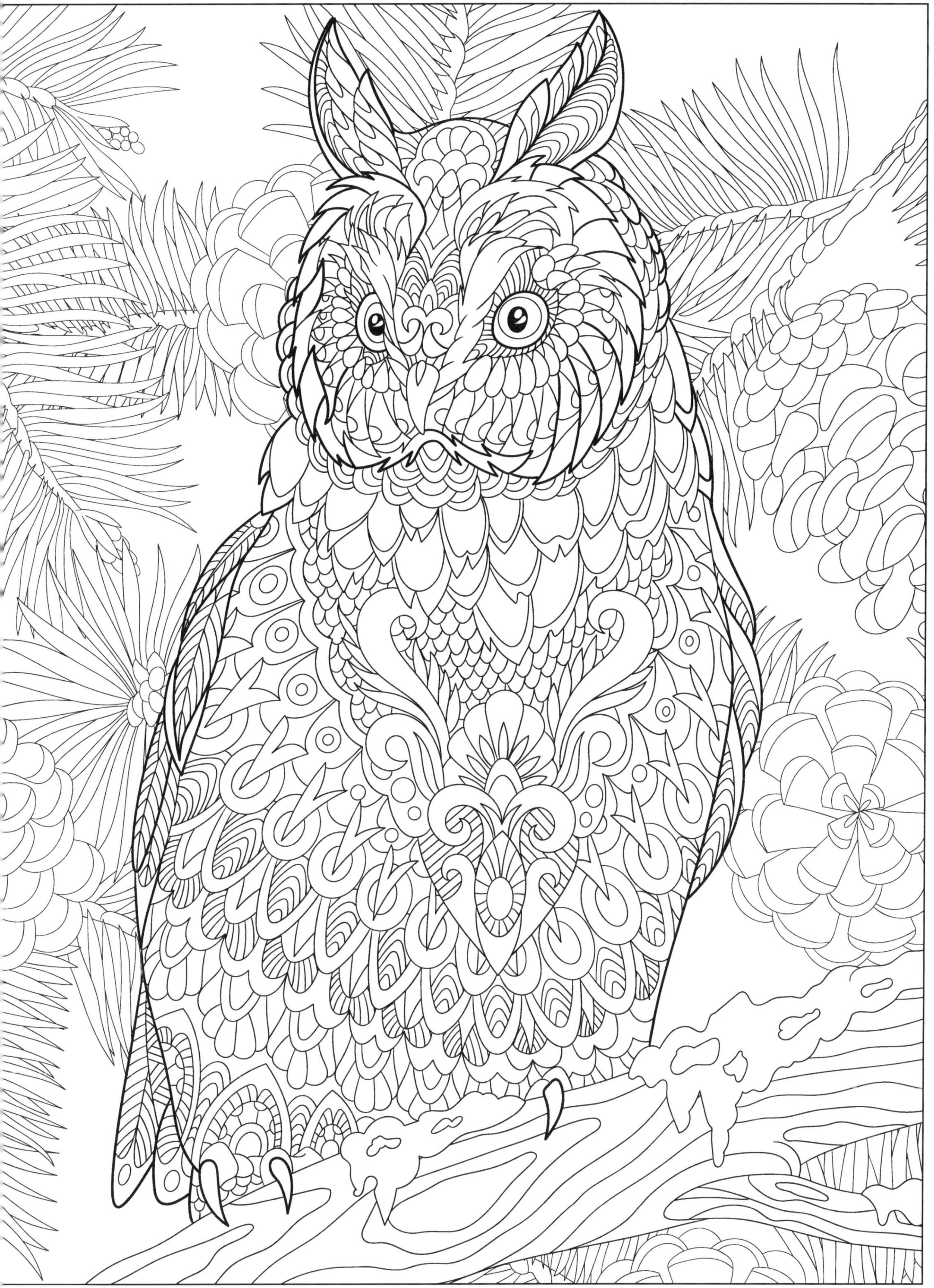

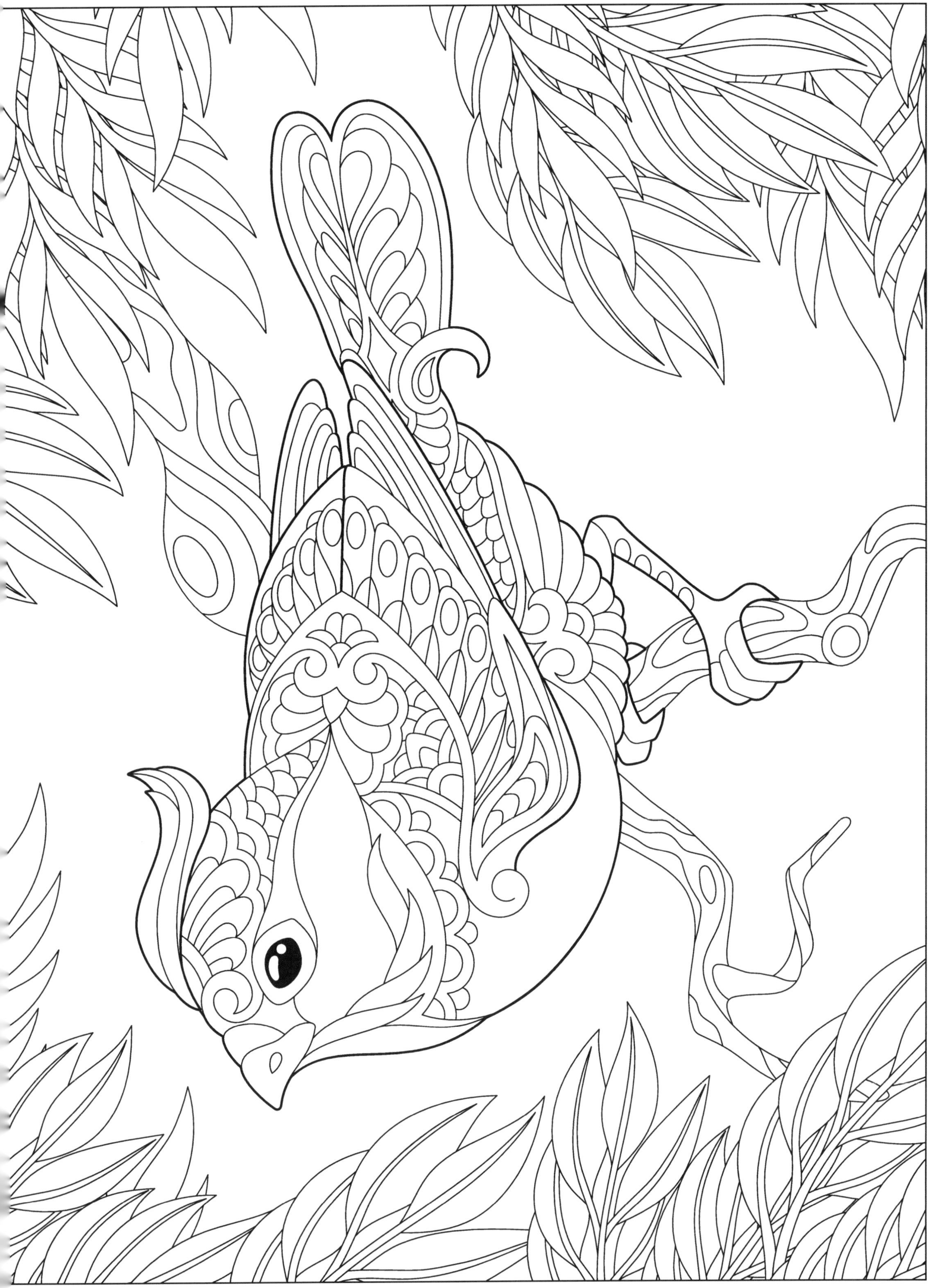

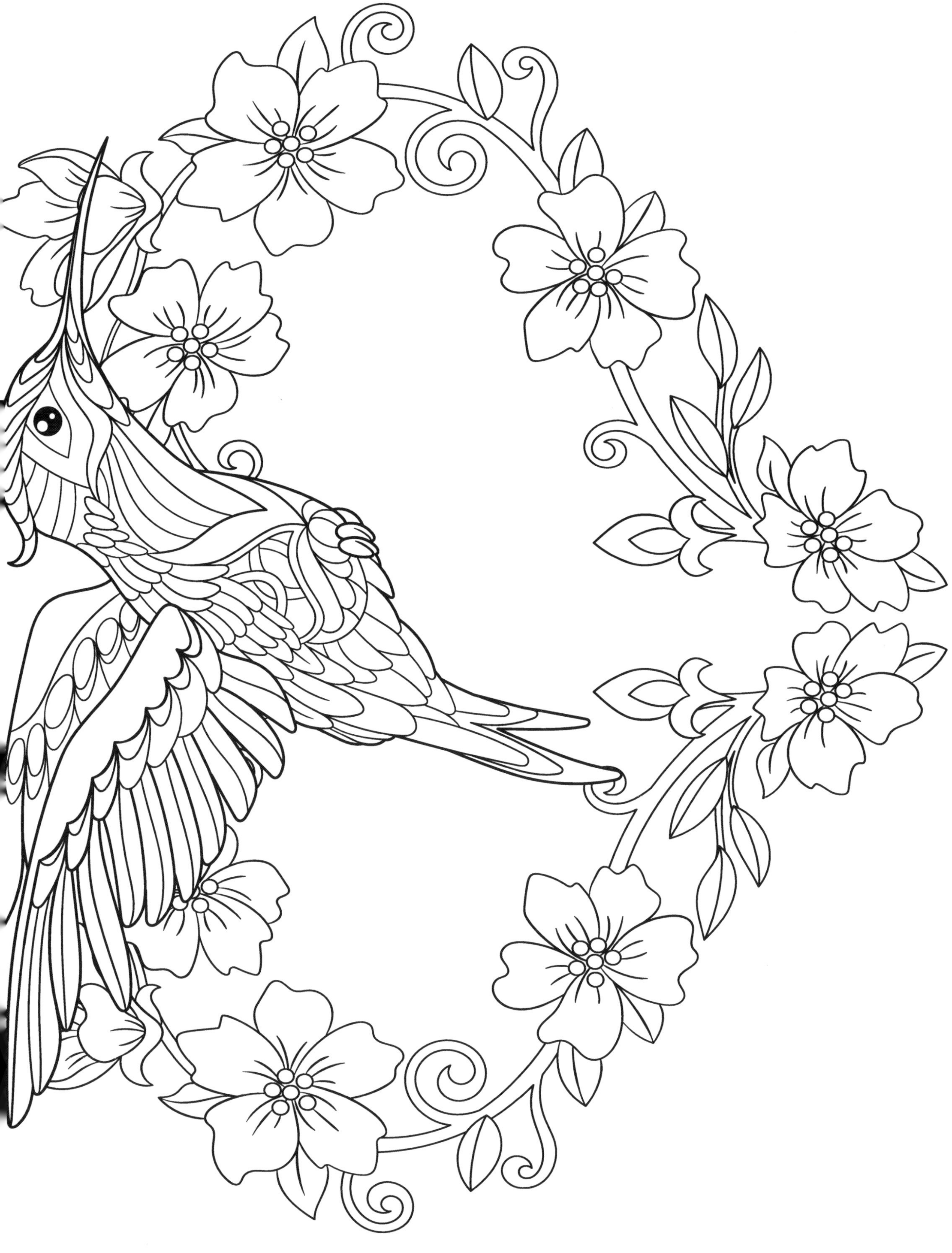

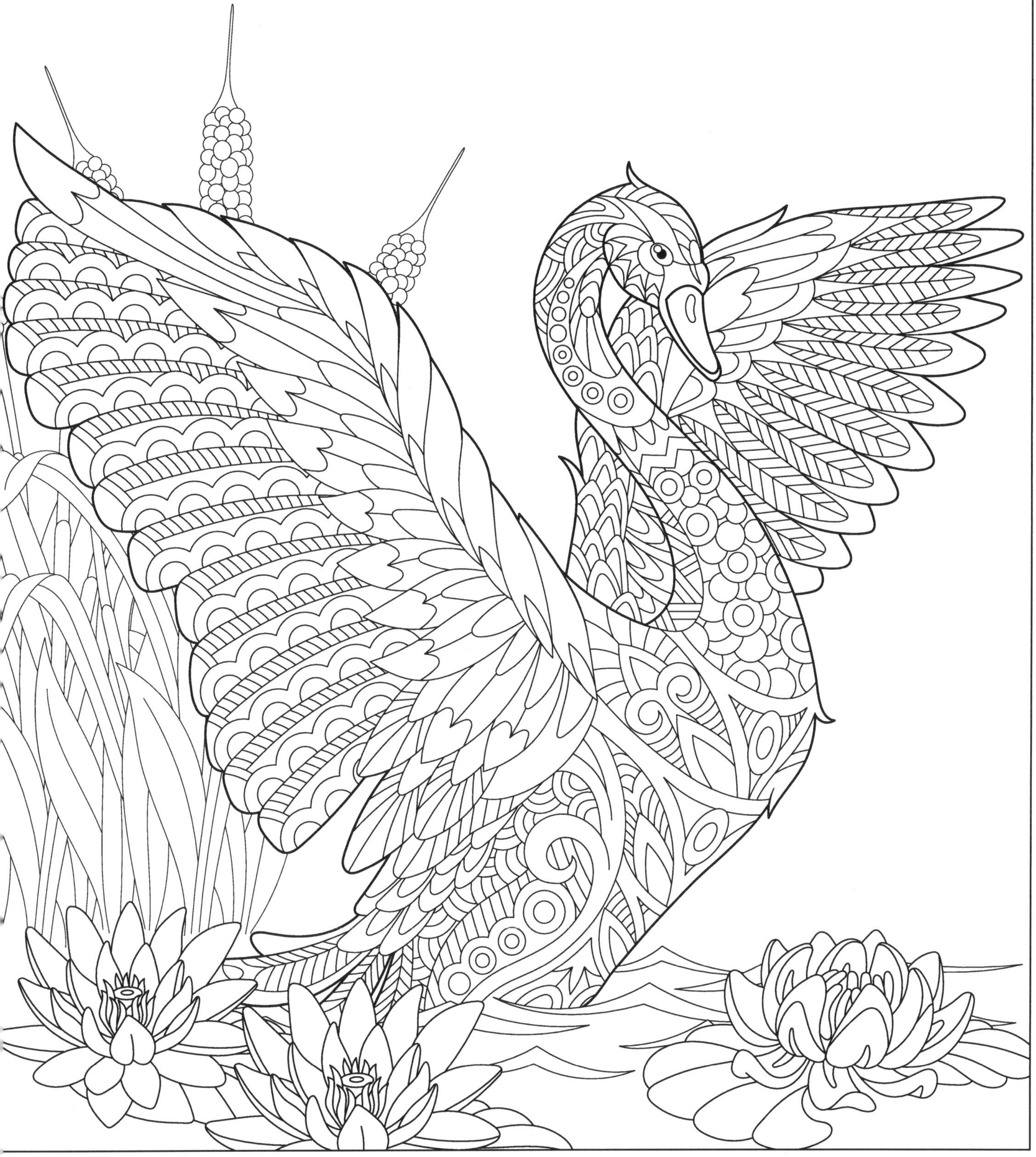

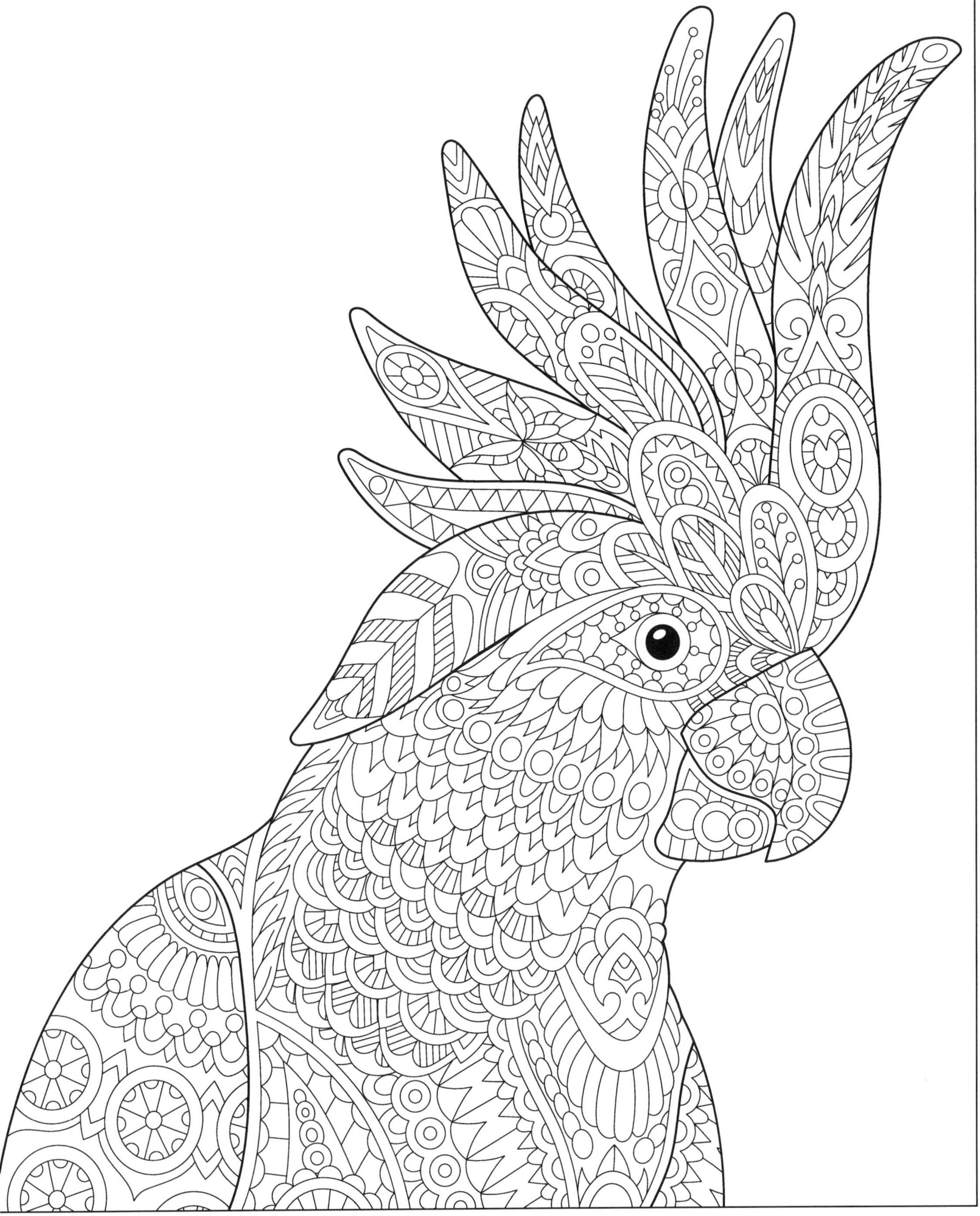

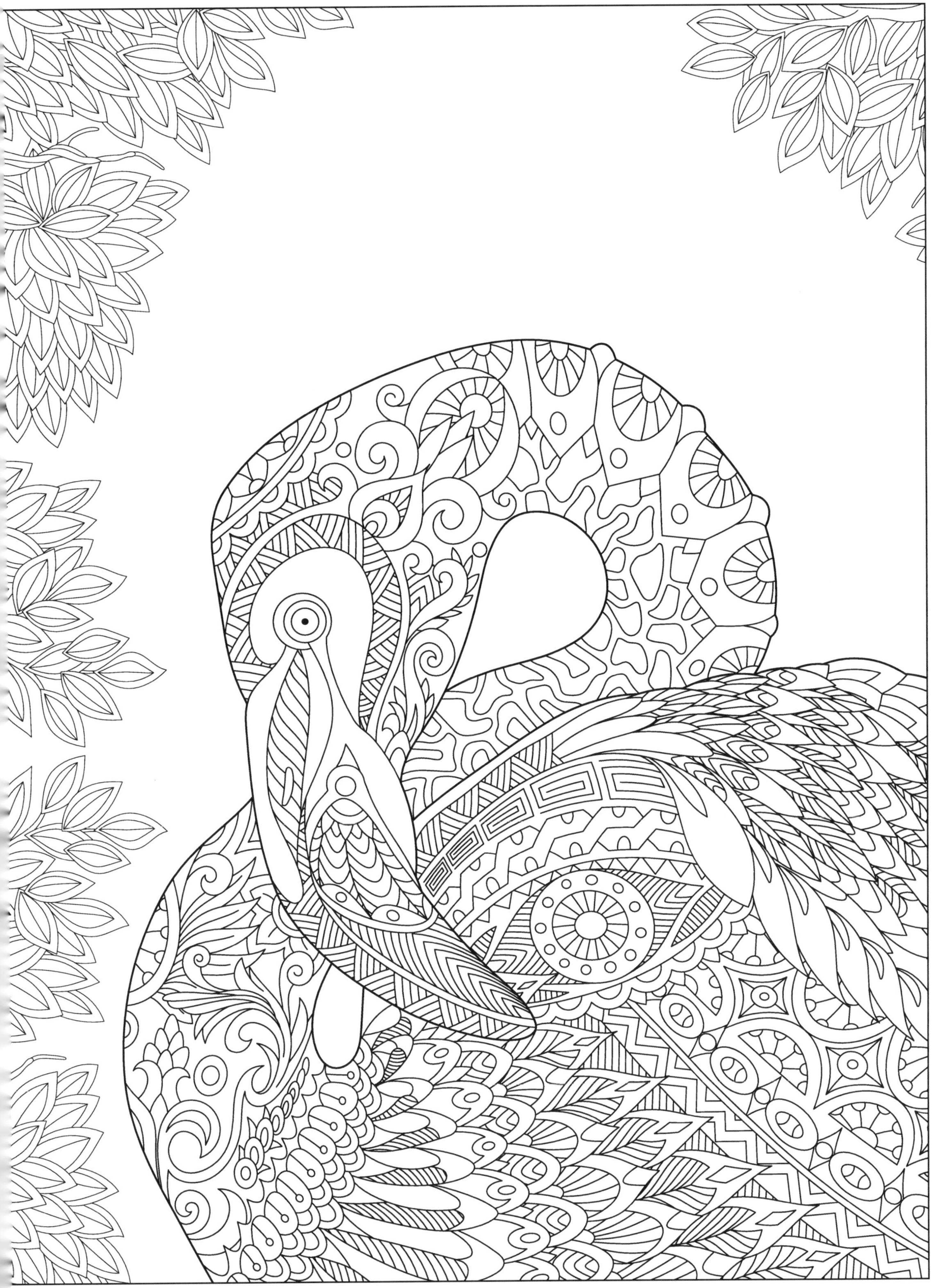

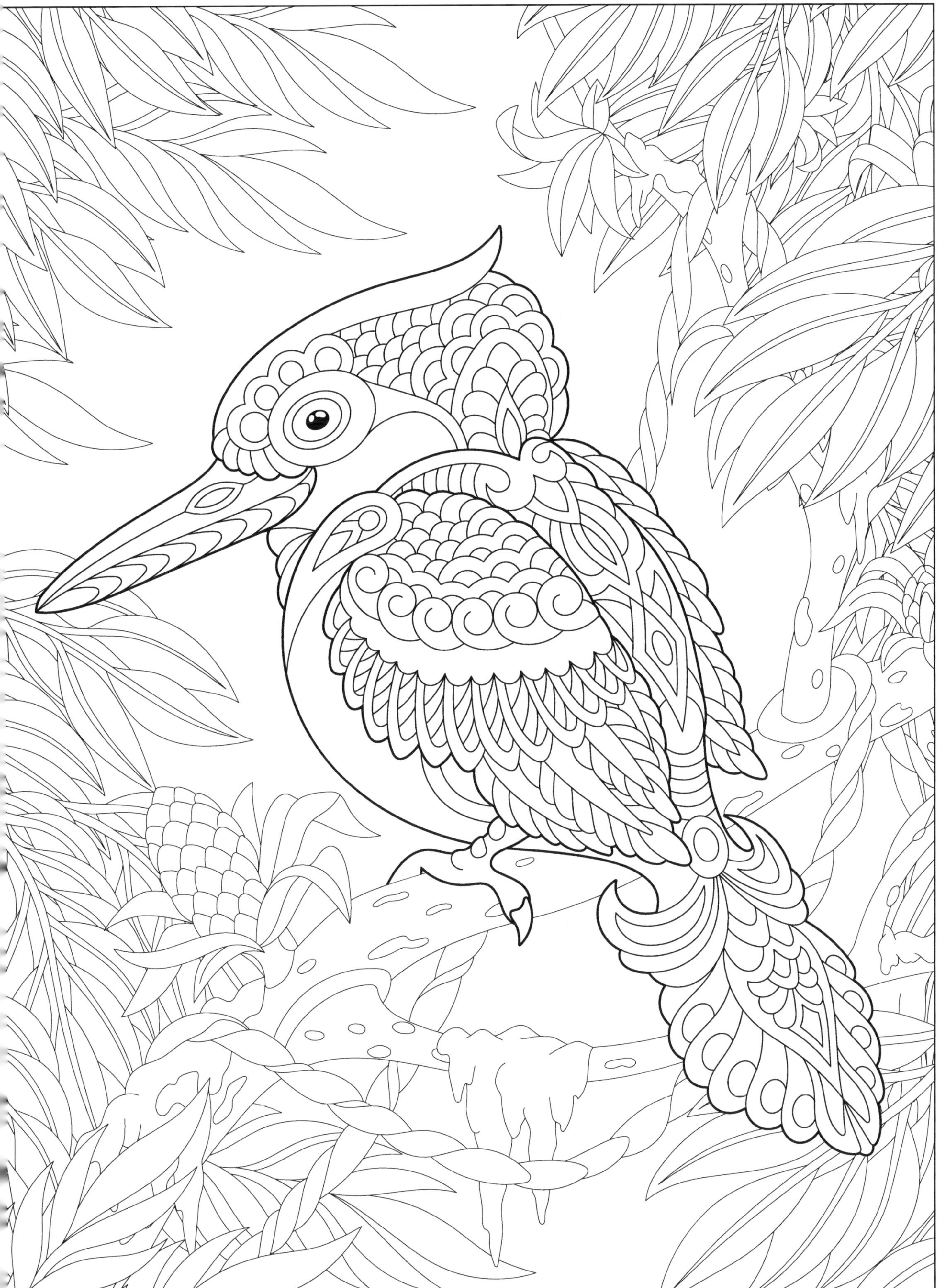

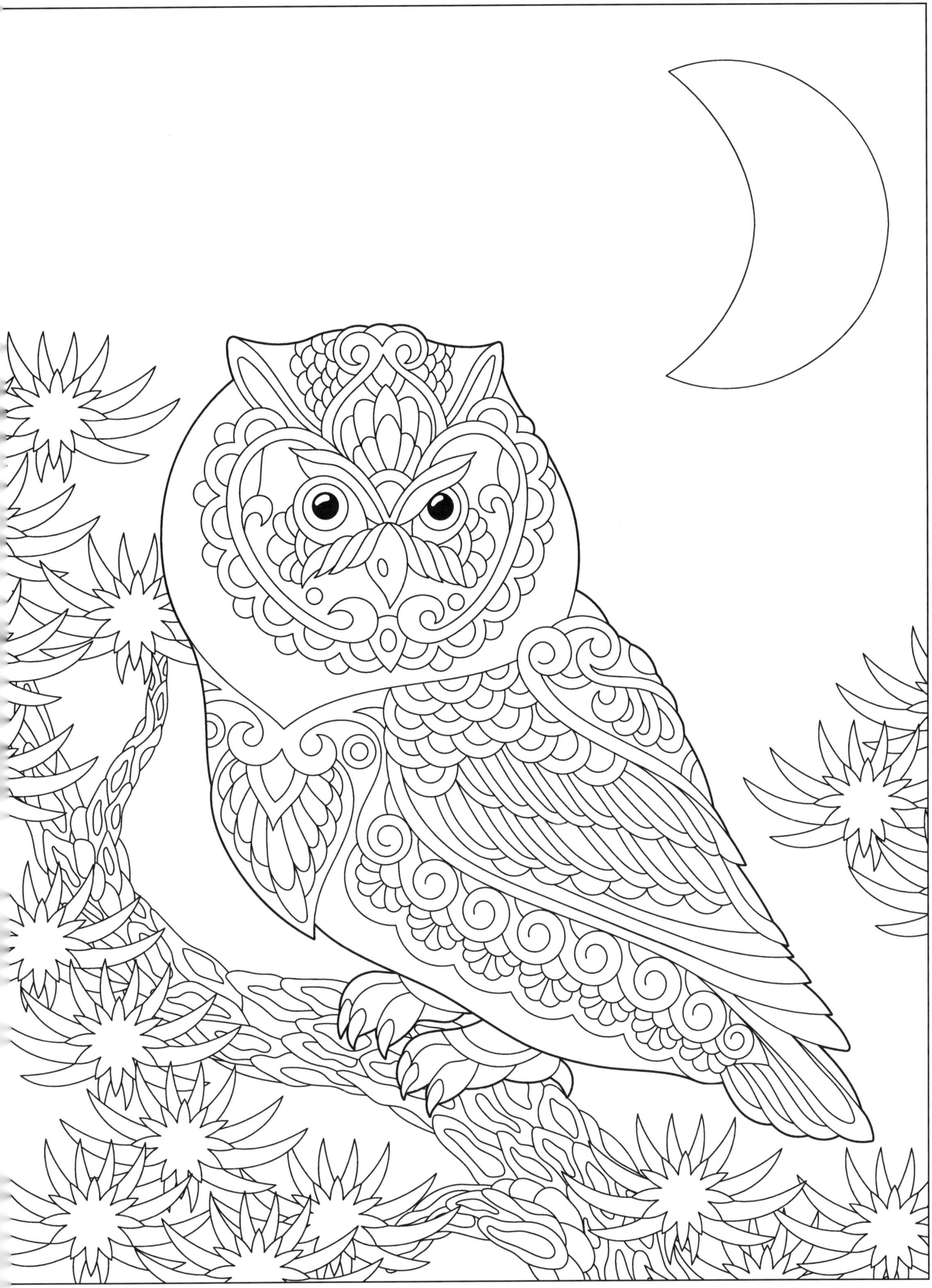

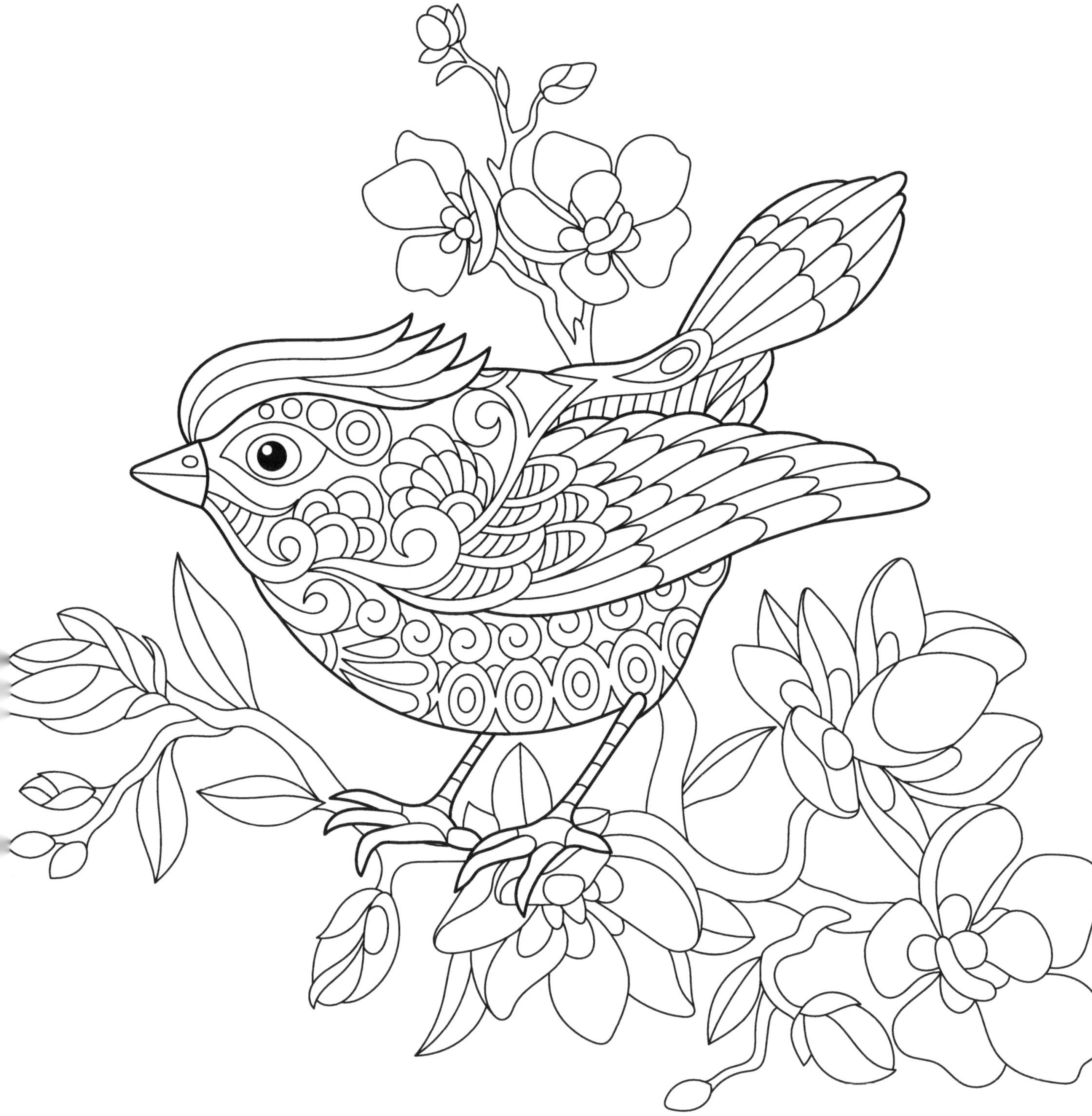

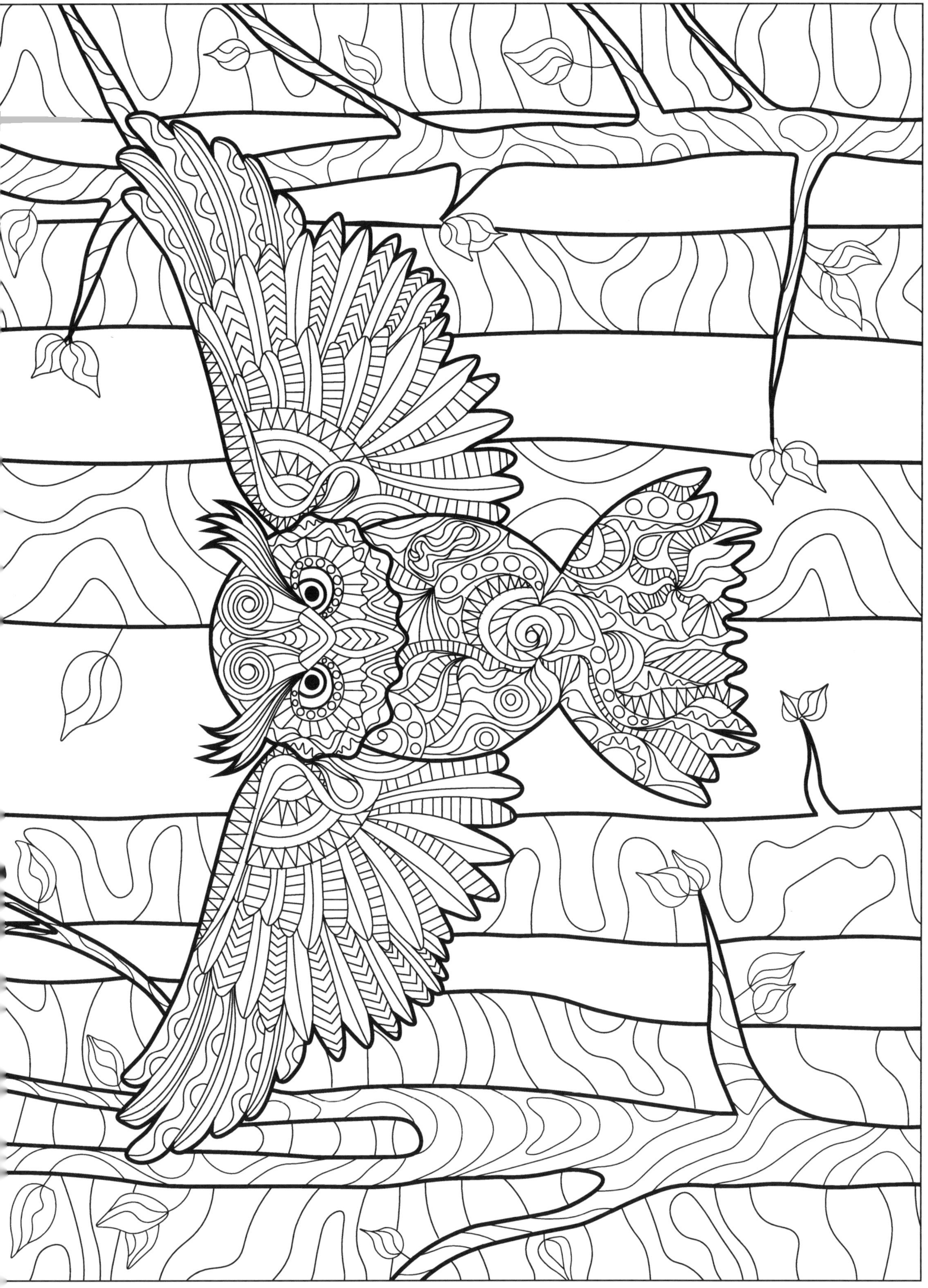

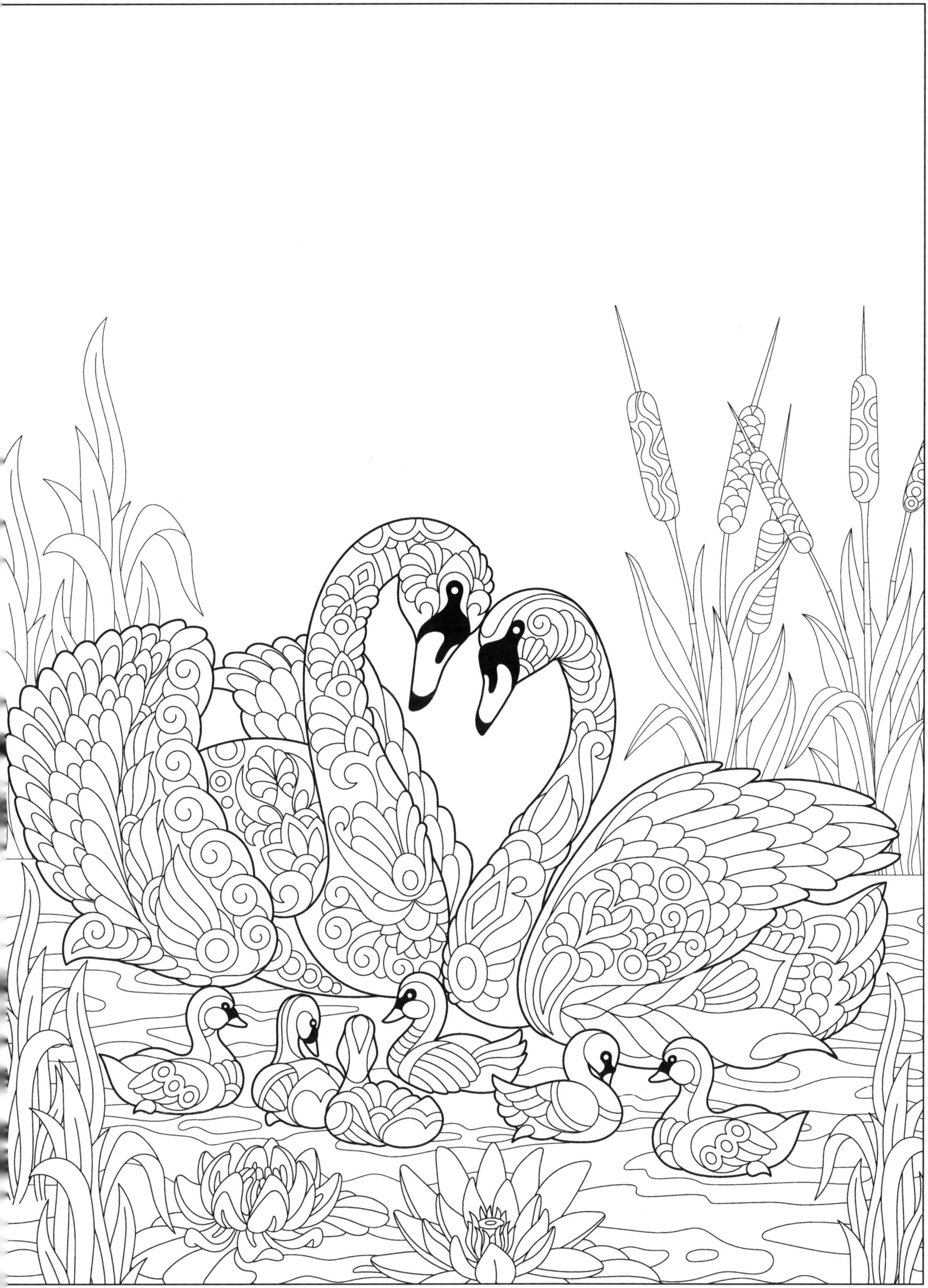

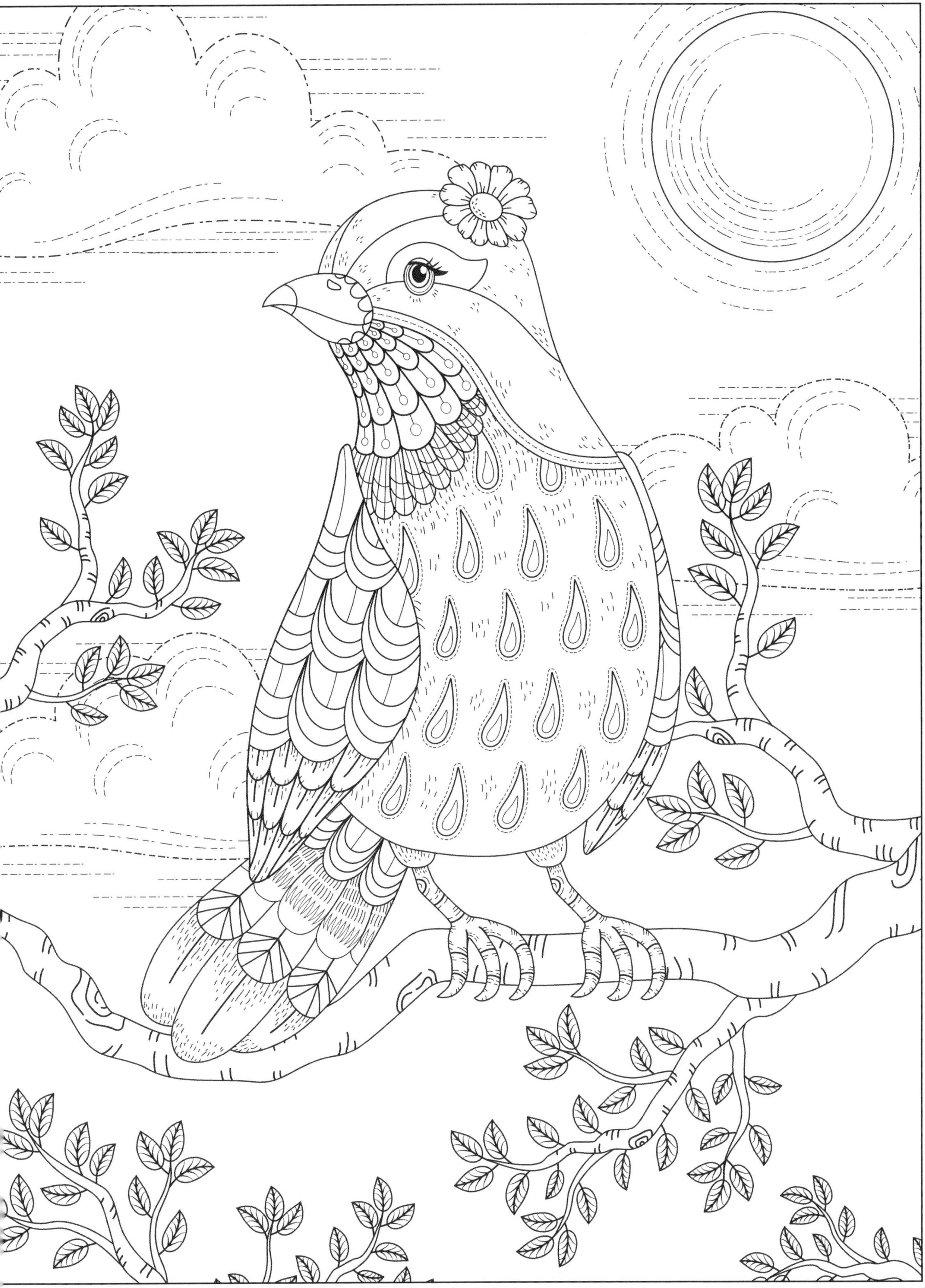

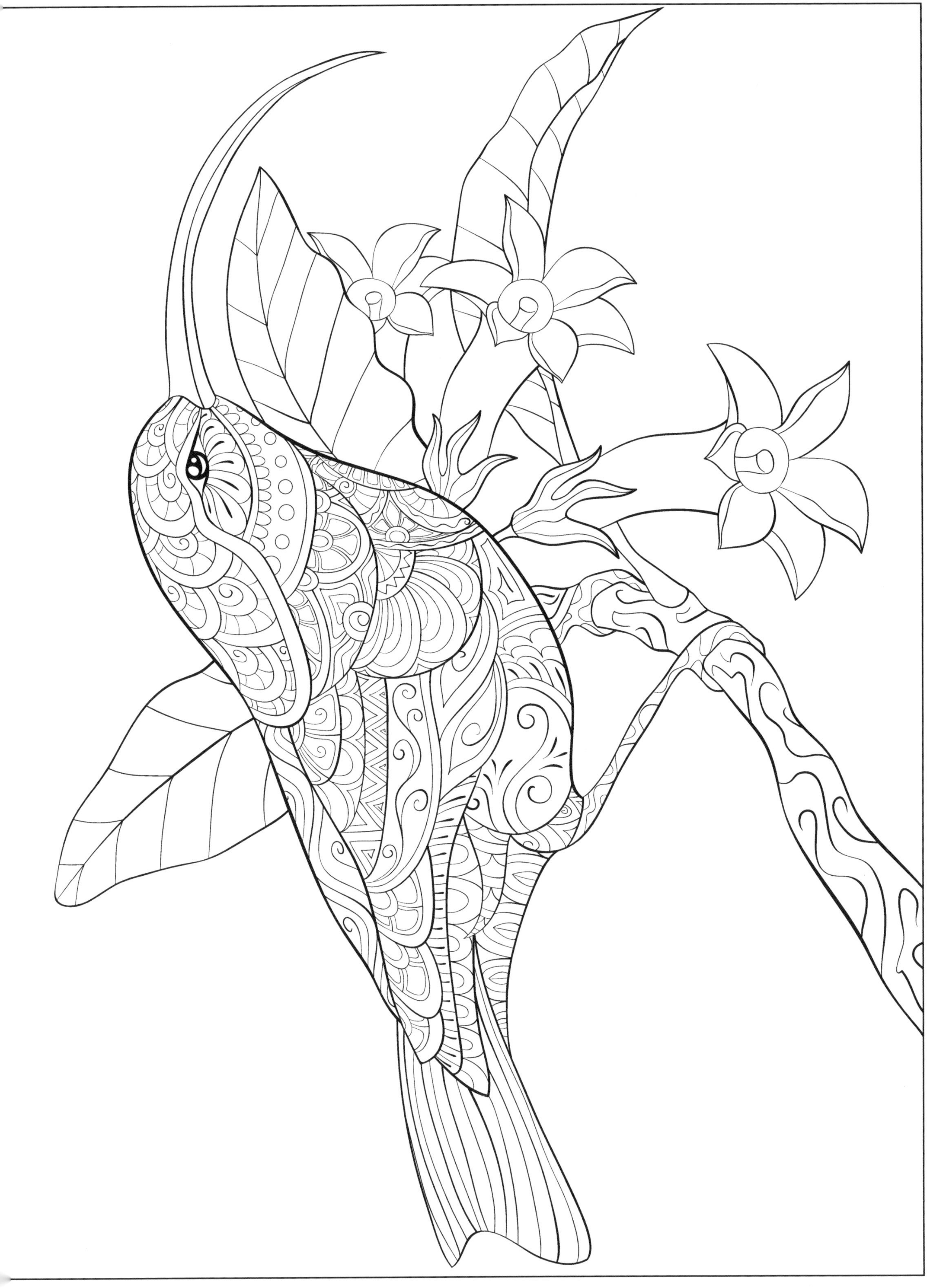

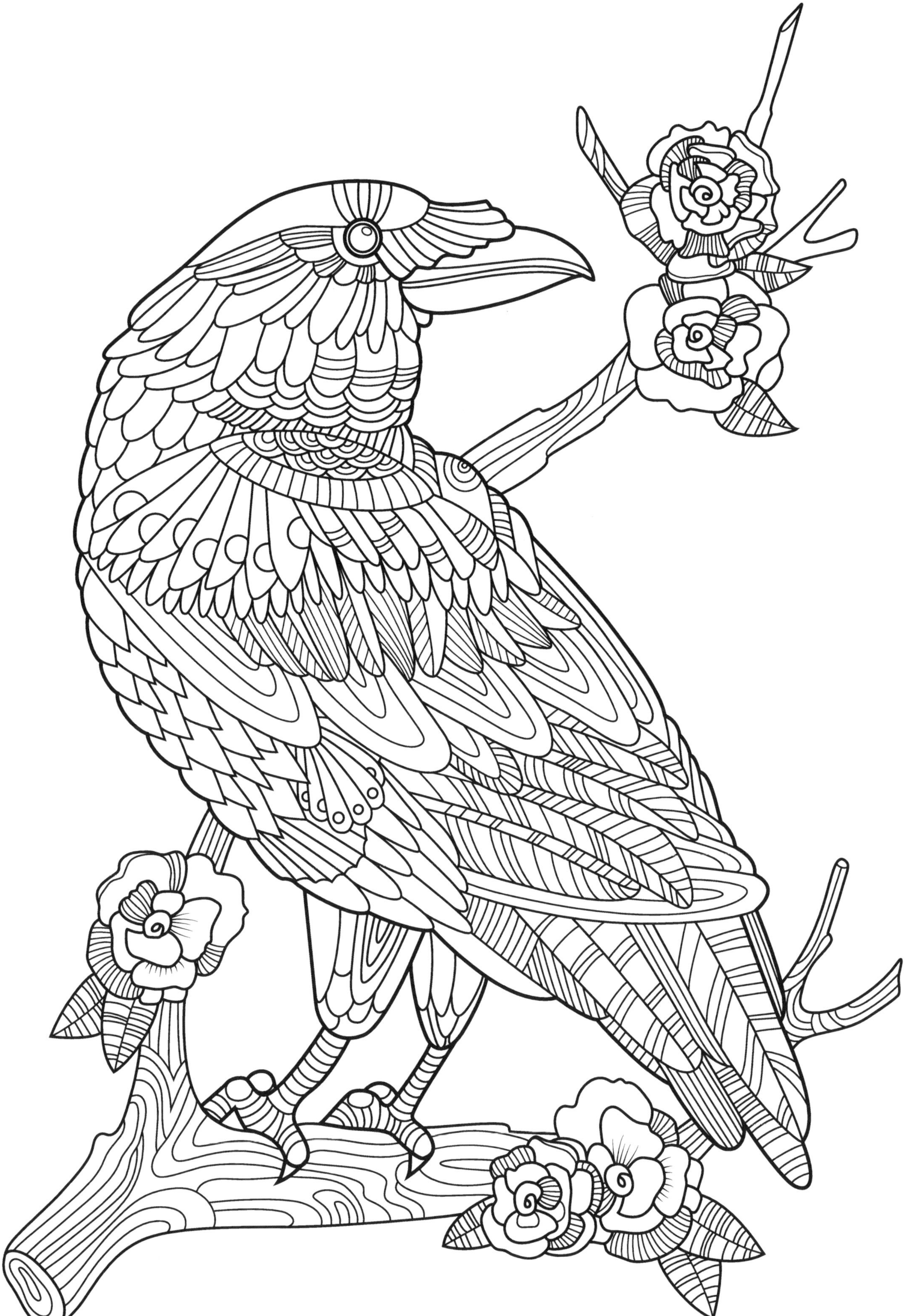

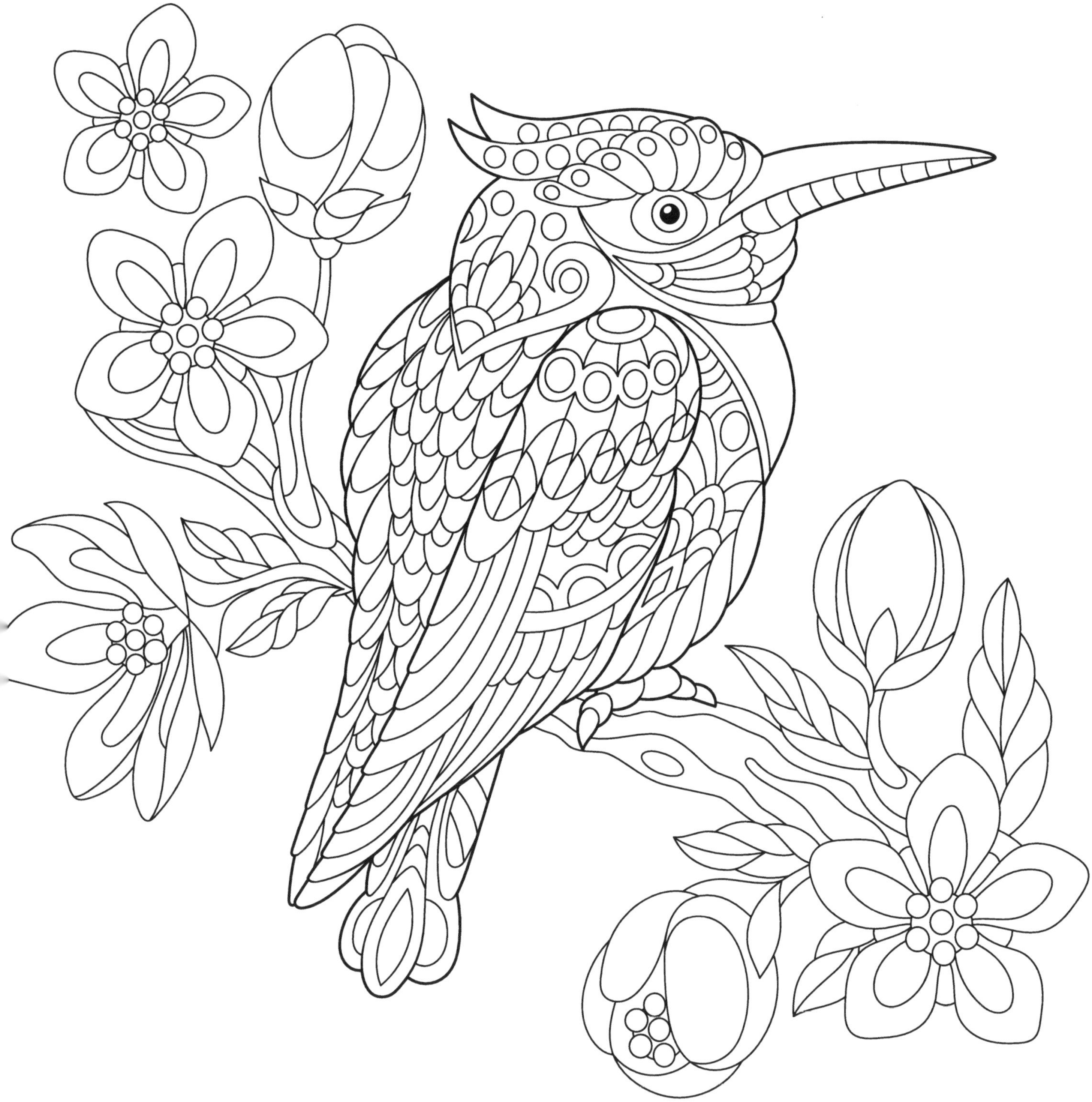

Made in the USA
Coppell, TX
09 April 2022

76226578R10061